A COMPLETE INTRODUCTION

LOVEBIRDS

A COMPLETE INTRODUCTION

Georg A. Radtke

Paintings of the wild forms and the color varieties of lovebirds by Eric Peake

Photographs: Glen S. Axelrod, 26, 68. Dr. Herbert R. Axelrod, 16, 31, 60, 64. S. Bischoff, 44. Michael Gilroy, 2-3, 12, 14, 34, 66, 67, 69. W. De Grahl, 33, 50, 74. A.J. Mobbs, 71. Horst Müller, 41, 70, 78, 84, 90. H. Reinhard, 13, 28, 29, 46, 53, 82, 94-95. Mervin F. Roberts, 63, 65. Courtesy of San Diego Zoo, 15, 51, 77. Vince Serbin, 25, 36. Tony Silva, 83. Louise Van der Meid, 20, 32, 37, 38. Dr. M. Vriends, 76, 91. Courtesy of Vogelpark Walsrode, 8, 9, 17, 18, 30, 42, 47, 48, 52, 54, 73, 80, 81, 88.

Based on *The T.F.H. Book of Lovebirds.*

© 1995 by T.F.H. Publications, Inc.

Distributed in the UNITED STATES to the Pet Trade by T.F.H. Publications, Inc., One T.F.H. Plaza, Neptune City, NJ 07753; distributed in the UNITED STATES to the Bookstore and Library Trade by National Book Network, Inc. 4720 Boston Way, Lanham MD 20706; in CANADA to the Pet Trade by H & L Pet Supplies Inc., 27 Kingston Crescent, Kitchener, Ontario N2B 2T6; Rolf C. Hagen Ltd., 3225 Sartelon Street, Montreal 382 Quebec; in CANADA to the Book Trade by Vanwell Publishing Ltd., 1 Northrup Crescent, St. Catharines, Ontario L2M 6P5 ; in ENGLAND by T.F.H. Publications, PO Box 15, Waterlooville PO7 6BQ; in AUSTRALIA AND THE SOUTH PACIFIC by T.F.H. (Australia), Pty. Ltd., Box 149, Brookvale 2100 N.S.W., Australia; in NEW ZEALAND by Brooklands Aquarium Ltd. 5 McGiven Drive, New Plymouth, RD1 New Zealand; in Japan by T.F.H. Publications, Japan—Jiro Tsuda, 10-12-3 Ohjidai, Sakura, Chiba 285, Japan; in SOUTH AFRICA by Lopis (Pty) Ltd., P.O. Box 39127, Booysens, 2016, Johannesburg, South Africa. Published by T.F.H. Publications, Inc.
MANUFACTURED IN THE UNITED STATES OF AMERICA
BY T.F.H. PUBLICATIONS, INC.

Contents

Introduction 8
Lovebirds With White Eye Rings 14
Masked Lovebirds 18
Fischer's Lovebirds 38
Nyasa Lovebirds 44
Black-cheeked Lovebirds 48
Species Without White Eye Rings 52
Peach-faced Lovebirds 54
Red-faced Lovebirds 70
Abyssinian Lovebirds 78
Black-collared Lovebirds 84
Gray-headed Lovebirds 88
Suggested Reading 92
Index 93

Introduction

Lovebirds are small parrots, about five to seven inches long. The nine known species *(Agapornis cana, A. fischeri, A. lilianae, A. nigrenis, A. personata, A. pullaria, A. roseicollis, A. swinderniana, A. taranta)* are natives of the savannah south of the Sahara desert in tropical Africa, an area which includes the island of Madagascar.

The name *Agapornis* (lovebird) comes from the Greek *(agapein,* to love; *ornis,* bird) and may well have originated with the first observers of these birds in their natural habitat. Even though these lively dwarf parrots fight on occasion and their life styles may differ from species to species, there is one characteristic they all have in common: they live in pairs all their lives. None will stray beyond calling distance of its mate. Except for breeding periods, lovebirds live

Above: *Peach-faced (lutino) lovebird.*

Above: *Peach-faced (wild coloration) lovebird.*

Below: *Masked lovebird.*

Below: *Peach-faced (pied-yellow-green) lovebird.*

Above: *Abyssinian male lovebird.*

Above: *Black-cheeked lovebird.*

Below: *Abyssinian female lovebird.*

Below: *Gray-headed (male) lovebird.*

together in sociable groups and often swarm in large numbers through the savannah, the fields, and the jungle. They rest in pairs, cuddling against each other. The partners enjoy grooming and feeding each other. "Marital spats" may be occasionally noisy, but almost always of brief duration.

Lovebirds are cavity breeders. In contrast to other cavity breeders, they carry nesting materials into the nesting hole and construct quite elaborate, tube-shaped breeding chambers. Most species select hollow trees for nesting places. Eggs are white—since they are laid in enclosed spaces, they do not require protective coloring. The females take care of most of the incubating, but the males also spend many hours daily in the nests. While the females are incubating, the males feed them from their crops. At night, they too sleep in the nesting cavity. Even when lovebirds are not raising young, knotholes and other protected places are favored for sleeping.

Lovebird babies are fed by both parents. Even after the young have left the nest, they continue to be provided with nourishment by their parents. If the hen is incubating a new clutch, the male often continues to feed the fledglings by himself. Mother Nature's table is richly set: seeds of many varieties of grasses, bushes, and trees; buds and seedlings; insects in all stages of their development; fruits and berries. Because of the high level of energy and liveliness of lovebirds, their appetites are usually excellent. Large flocks can cause considerable damage to grain fields and orchards.

Lovebirds need to be near water, as they drink often and love to bathe. Consequently, they seldom fly far from their watering places. Even though their flight is rapid and agile, their short wings keep

Above: *Peach-faced (red-flecked) lovebird.*
Below: *Dutch blue peach-faced lovebird.*

Above: *Black-cheeked (yellow) lovebird.*

Below: *Red-faced lovebird.*

Above: *Nyasa lovebird.*

Above: *Masked (blue) lovebird.*

Below: *Dutch blue ino peach-faced lovebird.*

Below: *Yellow peach-faced lovebird.*

them from extended flights. In addition, the periodical tropical droughts tend to limit long flights, as all energy and strength are focused on survival. Droughts affect not only the flying habits of the birds but also—and even more—their breeding instincts.

All these facts must be clearly understood before we acquire our first lovebirds, if we want to keep these children of the tropics happy, healthy, and—if possible—

breeding. This last is an obligation which we share more and more, in view of our increasingly impoverished environment. Growing numbers of countries regulate or even prohibit the exportation of their native fauna for whatever purposes. Up to the middle of this century, much damage was done, particularly in importing and exporting birds. Today's bird lover has to concentrate above all on breeding, for his own sake and that of others. We no

longer have the luxury of unlimited imports. Fortunately for us, our predecessors have borne the greatest burden, sometimes at great financial costs, since lovebirds were first imported at the beginning of the previous century. We owe an excellent summary to Hampe *(Die Unzertrennlichen,* 1957) who collected all available information and experience about the care and breeding early in this century. Since then, lovebirds have increased in popularity; in addition, the long domestication of many species is leading to many very interesting color mutations.

In this book, I am not necessarily following the established systematic

Above: *Peach-faced lovebirds, in their native habitat, live on steep, arid mountain cliffs on the edge of the desert.* Facing page: *Fischer's lovebirds are very sociable.*

arrangement; rather I will begin with those species which are most popular and most easily bred. For added ease in looking up information, I did not lump together care and feeding, diseases, and breeding idiosyncrasies in particular chapters, but distributed this information under the headings of the appropriate species. Where the requirements for several species are quite similar, reference is made to previously mentioned information.

I hope and trust that this handbook will contribute to a closer relationship between bird lovers on one side and the lovable Africans on the other.

GEORG A. RADTKE

Lovebirds with White Eye Rings

In the early days of raising and breeding lovebirds, there was a widespread conviction that the four species with white eye rings *(Agapornis fischeri, A. lilianae, A. nigrigenis, A. personata—* which all belong to the same group) were the easiest to keep and to breed. Further developments have shown that this is not necessarily true, or the numbers of these four species would logically be the greatest. A look at the map of their ranges shows how closely they lie together, indicating a relationship on a geographical basis. It is interesting to note that the species do not interbreed in the border regions, as happens frequently with other birds (like the carrion and hooded crows along the Elbe river or many

Fischer's lovebirds are just one of four species with white eye rings.

Australasian weaver finches). The simplest explanation for this is that the natural barriers found in the widely divergent African landscape of jungles, streams, and mountain ranges are formidable obstacles for the short wings of our little parrots. Of course, this no longer applies in their European refuge, the aviaries of the breeders. There the natural barriers are completely absent, as is the need for a daily struggle for food. Different species are deliberately brought into contact with each other, even though they may not have been acquainted before. The natural result has been

The lutino Nyasa lovebird is the smallest of the species with white eye rings.

interbreeding, with fertile offspring. These initially playful attempts of many amateur breeders have proven that the relationship between many species is indeed a close one, and that in many cases their development in separate directions may have been the result of geological upheavals.

To bring the species together again and to raise differently colored offspring may be quite attractive, but it may also result in an undefinable population mix, which theoretically may be quite similar to the original form. There are several examples of this in the history of animal breeding, designated by the term *atavism.* For the amateur

Due to their distinctive markings and coloring, masked lovebirds are considered by some to be the most attractive members of the genus.

breeder, this is of little importance, but it is diametrically opposed to the essential preservation of each species, toward which efforts are so vital today. With this in mind, the two largest German breeders' associations have removed lovebird hybrids from their classification system. Besides, the hybrid of a masked lovebird and a Fischer's lovebird is never as attractive as either of the pure species. In addition, it resembles the black-cheeked lovebird so closely that novices in the field could easily be deceived. Admittedly, the offspring of crosses between black-cheeked lovebirds with Nyasa lovebirds are very attractive, but the low numbers of pure-bred birds of these species prohibit this kind of manipulation. Crossbreeding is justified only if no partners of the same species are available and then the offspring must be declared to be a hybrid.

The four species with white eye rings differ only minimally from each other in their life styles and behavior. For instance, they all tend to carry the nesting materials in their

These black-cheeked lovebirds show some of the variation in coloration typical of this species.

bills; in captivity, they enjoy fresh willow twigs which they quickly split and interweave. Their nests are usually quite solid. Even in an enclosed nesting box, they do not forego a "roof," and the entrance to the nest is near the rear wall.

All in all, the species with white eye rings are less demanding and better adapted to a northern climate than the species without white eye rings. (For exceptions, please see the sections for particular species.)

Masked Lovebirds

Agapornis personata

Beyond a doubt, masked lovebirds are the most attractive members of the genus due to their distinctive markings and coloring. Males and females look almost identical and measure about five and three-quarters inches.

According to Forshaw *(Parrots of the World,* T.F.H. Publications, 1977) masked lovebirds live in grassy steppes interspersed with baobab trees and acacias, at altitudes of up to 5,000 feet. They breed in colonies, from March to August. Preferred nesting cavities are the knotholes of baobab trees, but the birds will nest in holes in walls, and even in abandoned swifts' nests. The females rarely lay clutches of more than four eggs. Masked lovebirds feed principally on the seeds of grasses and herbs, which they also pick off the ground while walking rapidly. Their flight is straight and quick, but not of long duration.

In captivity, a pair of masked lovebirds will be satisfied with a cage of about 32 by 16 inches, either all metal wire or a box cage of plastic. (A box cage is a simple box of wood, metal, or plastic, with wire mesh on the longest side.) Wooden cages are not very suitable for lovebirds, since they prove no match for their strong beaks.

If a metal wire cage is used, a nesting box should be fastened to the outside; with a box cage, it is better to attach the nesting box to the inside, since the birds feel more protected there. Modern plastic breeding cages are commercially available; they feature a door on the side and a board in the upper third on which the nesting boxes can be placed, which permit easy access for inspection

A masked lovebird hen incubating.

Masked lovebirds, as all lovebirds, have an enormous need for affection and company.

purposes. Roomy parakeet nesting boxes are recommended, 6 by 8 and about 10 inches tall, to allow the lovebirds to build a quite bulky nest. The entrance hole should be positioned in the upper part, to one side. It need not be bigger than 2 inches in diameter—masked lovebirds and related species will adapt it to their needs by gnawing it to the correct size. As always, everything that supports the birds' natural instincts will assist in breeding. This is why easily built wooden nesting boxes are best, even though they are not very durable. Perches on the boxes are not absolutely essential, but having one will facilitate the birds' entrance; also, the male likes to sit on it during the incubation period. Even at other times, the parent birds like to use the nesting box as a place to sleep. It is wise, however, to remove this cozy

Masked lovebirds kept in pairs are generally much stronger and disease resistant than singly-kept birds.

The blue masked lovebird. The blue coloring is a trait recessive to the normal green color.

sleeping place, as the birds tend to become stimulated to more frequent breeding than their constitution can deal with. After two or three successful breedings, the nesting box should be removed for several months to give the birds a chance to recover fully and to regain their strength. Without this precaution, their life expectancy is shortened, and the health of each succeeding brood decreases until no viable offspring are produced.

People who keep just one pair of lovebirds as

companions in a warm apartment and are not interested in offspring should remove the nesting box altogether. What the birds don't know, they won't miss. Incidentally, for almost all cavity breeders, the nesting box is the strongest trigger for breeding. If it is absent, the hen will rarely lay.

If you are not disturbed Supervision is necessary for the sake of furniture and drapes. Masked lovebirds also need to be protected from exposure to poisonous houseplants; highly curious, they gnaw at everything. Special treats, such as ears of spray millet or greens, will bring them back to the cage.

Lovebirds hand-raised

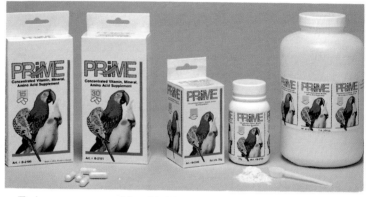

To be sure your pet lovebird is receiving a complete and well-balanced diet, include a vitamin and mineral supplement. Powder and capsule forms are available from your local pet shop. Photo courtesy of Hagen Products.

by their somewhat shrill cries, you will enjoy these delightful roommates, who can become quite tame and confident if they are allowed free flight through the rooms, adequately supervised. They will soon become very clever, returning regularly to their cage, as long as they are never fed anywhere else.

from a very early age can become extremely tame and friendly, since the normal close attachment to parents and siblings is transferred to the human. A person who likes tame, single birds and is fortunate to obtain a hand-raised specimen should therefore be prepared to assume a great deal of responsibility. These charmers are called lovebirds, or "inseparables," not by accident, and their need for affection and company, focused on their human, is enormous. Many of these birds even learn to repeat a few words or to whistle. They should not be left alone for any length of time; this makes them suitable only for families in which some member is always home, or for people with lots of free time. Others should not consider getting a lovebird, because lack of company may lead to bad habits such as feather plucking, or even to illness and early death.

From about the third week on, when the quills begin to break through and the babies no longer need quite as much warmth,

Spray millet is especially liked by lovebirds. This nutritious and fun-to-eat treat is available at a pet store near you. Photo courtesy of Hagen Products.

A white masked lovebird gathering willow twigs for nest building. Although both partners are involved in the nest construction, it is characteristic for the female to collect the material.

young masked lovebirds can be fed by hand with a warm millet gruel, to which calcium supplements and vitamins have been added. The little birds learn quickly to accept their food from the end of a small spoon. (Let me explain here that I do not in principle advocate the hand-raising of young birds. However, it happens frequently that breeders are forced into this position through default—for whatever reasons—on the part of the parent birds.)

Masked lovebirds kept in pairs or larger groups are much stronger and more disease-resistant than are singly-kept hand-raised birds, unless gross mistakes are made in their care. They do get occasional colds or upset stomachs. These illnesses are quite quickly and simply healed with appropriate medication, diet (millet spray, oatmeal), and warmth (heat lamp). Injuries on feet and legs (from fighting birds who bite each other) normally heal quickly; in the case of inflammations, antibiotic powders and such are indicated. Nails and toes lost to frostbite, bites, or other injuries, however, cannot be replaced! Lovebirds seem to have a tendency towards this type of injury because of their fleshy feet, which they injure not only in fights with rival birds, but by hanging on the aviary mesh during periods of frost. For this reason alone, lovebirds should be kept in temperatures well above freezing, although a mild frost is otherwise not harmful to them. The ideal environment is an aviary setting with large frost-free rooms that can be closed off. (In northern climates, these protected rooms should be larger than the outdoor flight areas.)

Lovebird perches should vary in diameter and offer the opportunity for exercise, climbing, and gnawing.

Masked Lovebird

Access to the outdoor sections should be by means of hatches, easily opened or closed according to weather and temperature. In such large enclosures several pairs of masked lovebirds can be permitted to breed at once.

These guidelines should be followed when breeding lovebirds in captivity: (1) Use only true pairs. (2) Do not keep more than one pair per cubic yard. (3)

Provide more nesting boxes than pairs, with all boxes of the same size and attached at the same level in the upper third of the enclosed room, in such a manner that they can easily be monitored without disturbing the breeding birds.

A lovebird aviary should contain, as this one does, several perches, nest boxes, and a feeding station.

With such an installation, much enjoyment and breeding success will be assured. You will be able to watch the birds display their charms—caressing, fighting, scolding and chasing each other, and in the next moment sharing food and bath.

Food and water containers should be sufficiently large and numerous. Water dishes will also be used for bathing and, therefore, should be rather shallow, but wide. As all dishes should be positioned so that they will not be soiled from the perches, feeding boards on the insides of doors are particularly handy. Even easier to care for are automatic dispensers for water and food. Make sure that only completely dry seed is used, as these clog easily. Automatic dishes must be cleaned and checked frequently, and an additional bathing dish will be needed. Cuttlebone and mineral blocks, both essential for the calcium requirements of lovebirds, are easily fastened to the mesh with wire. Galvanized spot-welded wire mesh seems most suitable (see Enehjelm, *Cages and Aviaries,* T.F.H. Publications, 1981).

In order to give the birds sufficient room for flight, not too many perches should be installed. If at all possible, perches should be of various diameters in order to exercise the birds'

Seed hoppers are easy to use but should be cleaned frequently, as they can clog easily.

feet and their leg muscles. A "climbing tree"—for instance, the lopped-off crown of a dwarf fruit tree with many twigs and branches—is a most welcome opportunity for exercise, climbing, and gnawing. (When you keep lovebirds, you had better get used to the idea that everything made of wood will need to be replaced quite frequently!)

The basic diet consists

of good budgerigar mix with a good amount of canary seed, including small striped sunflower seeds and a little hemp, which is augmented according to the season with greens, various weed seeds, half-ripe grass panicles and ears of corn. For breeding birds, we recommend a good commercial nestling food, enriched with mashed egg yolk and grated apples or carrots. Make sure the parrots become used to

The first blue-white masked lovebirds were bred in England.

this diet even before the young are hatched. Not all pairs will accept this kind of food; others prefer crumbled dog biscuits or dog food, fruit, and berries. This is a matter of trial and error, with success the decisive factor, not the means by which it was achieved. Once you have found an acceptable menu, you should stick with it.

For fresh greens, particularly in winter, sprouting the various seeds has proven successful (use a separate dish for each variety). Commercially available sprouting dishes make this simple process partially foolproof. In winter, the drinking water should be enriched at regular intervals by the addition of liquid vitamins. Sick birds may need to be fed one vitamin drop daily in the throat for three successive days, with a plastic eye dropper. This also may prove successful with birds which are reluctant to breed. Once all preparations have been made, the breeding pairs may then move in.

This raises a problem which has caused many a headache among bird lovers: distinguishing the sexes. Many authors cite various external sex distinctions among masked lovebirds and related species, but none has proven completely accurate. Probably the most obvious test is to compare fully-grown birds by size; females of this group of lovebirds are usually larger and heavier—but not without exception. It is fortunate that when the lovebirds can be observed in a group and can be selected accordingly, individual pairs can soon be discerned by their behavior. In a cage, two birds may behave like a pair even though they are of the same sex.

The most accurate method of sexing the birds is by palpation of the pelvic bones from the sternum downward. The pelvic bones of a fully grown male are close together, whereas there is a space of several millimeters between the pelvic bones of a sexually mature female. The use of this method requires a gentle finger tip and practice. The novice should be instructed in its use by an experienced breeder.

A "dubious" pair should not be put into the aviary, because the imbalance of pairs will cause brood-disturbing fights from the

The yellow masked lovebird is believed to have been bred first in Japan.

very beginning.

If everything goes according to plan, the pairs should soon begin to build a nest. Both partners are involved in its construction, although it is usually the female who collects the material. You should give the birds a wide choice of nesting materials. Fresh willow twigs are the most suitable; if those are not available, other twigs (of

The coloration on the yellow masked lovebird is not pure, as it is tinged with green.

nonpoisonous plants!) will do. Twigs are best put into a sturdy and sufficiently large container filled with water.

Once the nest is ready, the female begins to lay her eggs. They usually lay three to seven eggs at two-day intervals. Incubation lasts from twenty-one to twenty-three days. Many females begin to incubate as soon as the first egg is laid, while others wait for one or two more. Usually, those babies that hatch two days late are just as well taken care of as the others. The young are covered with a pinkish down, which later is replaced by a gray down; this remains until their colorful feathers begin to grow.

Lovebird chicks are hatched blind; they open their eyes on about the tenth day. After about forty-three days, the fledglings leave the nest. Their feathers are fully grown, and even though their plumage is still youthfully pale, it already shows the distinctive markings and coloration of mature birds. Healthy youngsters fly well from the beginning and are quite capable of feeding themselves, but they are fed for a while longer, usually by the male. By this time, the hen is usually busy with her next clutch.

Once the young birds are on their own, an especially careful watch must be kept on the other birds in the aviary. As soon as there are any indications of dangerous biting—just when is unpredictable—the young birds must be separated from the old. This is one reason why a serious breeder of lovebirds cannot make do with one flight; he needs to have at least two available.

During the warm season, though the young birds need no sleeping boxes, they will be grateful for some boards in the upper third of the protected rooms so that they may rest their still-weak legs while sleeping. For the

Bathing will keep your pet lovebird's plumage in optimum condition. There are many different styles of baths available from your local pet store. Photo courtesy of Hagen Products.

related species that winter in cold temperatures should be given sleeping boxes without nesting material and, if possible, should be kept separated according to sex. This will keep the females from laying. An occasional "lost" egg is no tragedy, even though the health of young females in very cold rooms may be endangered by egg binding. Pairs that have bred two or three times during the summer season should be separated from the breeding colony and kept

owner of an outdoor aviary, the best time for breeding is during the warm season. The angle of the sun's rays, the availability of greens, etc., are to his advantage. Winter breeding is successful only in well-heated indoor rooms. Masked lovebirds and

in a manner similar to young birds.

When breeding masked lovebirds in single pairs in box cages having a minimum length of 40 inches (or better, 50 to 60 inches), many of these problems will be avoided. Perhaps birds used to an aviary will be slower to breed, but breeding will go more smoothly. Nest inspection, individualized feeding, and cleaning are easier. For this reason, many breeders are switching to breeding in separate cages, although more work is involved with this method. The amount of time involved should not be underestimated: it takes time to establish a certain routine. Therefore, it is much better to begin small

Ground corn cob is frequently used as a floor covering.

with one or two pairs. Those who do not wish too much expense at first will enjoy their hobby more by beginning modestly and growing with the earnings from selling the offspring, reinvesting the money earned and the experience gained.

Large box cages with removable interior partitions are especially recommended. Such cages can easily be adapted as flight cages for the young and resting birds, since lovebirds do not require large outdoor aviaries. Unlike budgerigars and other parakeets, lovebirds do not care much for long-distance flights. This is indicated by their build: short tail and wings. Of course, it is good for young and resting birds to have the opportunity to fly in light, air, and sun, or showering in the rain but it is not absolutely necessary. For this reason, masked lovebirds and similar species can successfully breed in the city, without the availability of outdoor aviaries. All that is needed is a bright, dry basement or attic room that can be adequately lit (with wide-spectrum fluorescents, for instance), heated (with economical electrical units), and aired (ventilator, hygrometer). Adequate humidity is a must, since lovebird eggs hatch perfectly only in a humidity of 65% or better (hence the hygrometer). The use of water dishes with large surfaces (even aquariums), regular sprinkling of the floor (which is best constructed of easily cleaned concrete), and care for constantly fresh nesting materials will prevent any problems.

Separate cages are an absolute requirement for color-selective breeding, since in most species of lovebirds color mutations appear to correspond to those found in budgerigars, immensely enriching our hobby!

The first blue masked lovebirds were bred in England, descending, according to Hampe (Die Unzertrennlichen, 1967), from a wild blue captured in Tanganyika in 1927. As was to be expected, this was a recessive trait from the wild green coloring. Thus pure green x blue will result in all green young, independent of sex, which, however, are all split to blue; matings with each other will produce 25% blue offspring. Split-to-blue x blue will bring forth 50% blue. Blue x blue will give

The orange coloring of some masked lovebirds was once thought to be an indication of age, but this is apparently not so.

100% blue, since the blues are pure. This allowed them to be bred rather quickly. At this time, they are only slightly more expensive than the green, after which they are certainly the most attractive variety. If blues continue to be bred with blues only, after some generations size will suffer. At this point, or preferably before, healthy wild birds should be bred back into the line. This is the entire secret of these mutations.

Nobody knows exactly when the first yellow appeared. It seems likely that the Japanese were the first to breed them. From there, these birds came to Europe, maybe ten but no longer than twenty years will tell whether it is possible to obtain a purer yellow, as this mutation is still quite recent.

Once there were blue and yellow birds, the breeding of white masked lovebirds was only one

ago. Their color is not pure yellow but faintly suffused with green. Their recessive inheritance follows the same rules as that of the so-called yellow budgerigars that have a green tinge. Their masks are not black, but brownish gray, mixed with red, which occasionally leads to their mistaken identification as peach-faced lovebirds. A hybrid of these species, however, never shows this much yellow. The future

A blue masked lovebird gathering nesting material. The bill securely holds the twigs, and rarely are any dropped.

step removed: just as white, blue-tinged budgerigars were bred from blue x yellow, Mendel's laws of heredity lead us to expect one blue-white offspring in sixteen from a blue x yellow pair. These birds are predominantly bluish white, with a light gray head and an almost white beak. With their pastel coloration, they are quite attractive in their way. Since they breed recessively to yellow, it is worthwhile to breed them within the same stock, particularly since these two colors enhance each other.

We also know of masked lovebirds that show a strong orange coloring instead of yellow. Even the head feathers may be underlaid with this color, without necessarily indicating a crossing with a black-cheeked lovebird. Hampe knew about these birds, but he mistakenly identified this coloration as a sign of age. In fact, young birds exhibiting these attractive colors are known today. Since there is no geographical separation between races in the wild, this strong coloration is probably a result of natural selection. However, it cannot properly be called a direct mutation.

For exhibition, all lovebirds are shown individually in internationally approved budgerigar show cages. The birds are evaluated by qualified judges, according to a prescribed point system, winning places according to quality and, if necessary, size, and earning ratings from "satisfactory" to "excellent."

As a proof of breeding standards, [in Germany] birds which are exhibited must be banded. The official diameter of the band is 4.5mm for all lovebirds. This legally required banding is no small problem. For various reasons, banding the birds with closed rings, such as can be obtained through membership in a breeders' association, is the best method. In addition to the breeder's membership number and a running number from 001 on, the

The banding of lovebirds, done when they are ten to twelve days old, is accomplished by first sliding the band over the two front toes and pushing it up the leg. Then the rear toes are pulled free.

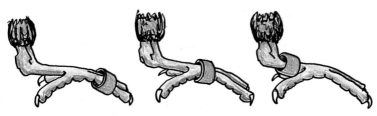

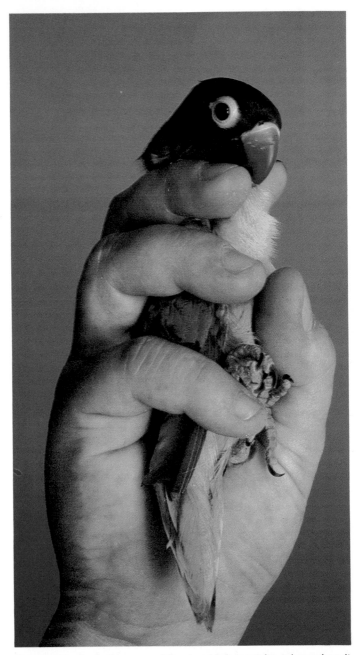

Great care, for both you and the lovebird, must be taken when it is necessary to handle it. Restrain the head between the second and third fingers. Lovebirds measure about five and three-quarters inches.

Distinguishing the sexes of lovebirds can be less difficult if they can be observed in a group. Pairs can be discerned by their behavior.

information contained on the ring includes the year, so that the bird's age is verifiable throughout its life, whether the bird is exhibited or not. This is always an advantage when buying and selling. Babies banded at an age of ten to twelve days become completely adjusted to the rings, so that they will not attempt to remove them later on. But with open rings, such as the central association of German pet dealers has issued as officially recognized rings for non-organized breeders, there is always the danger of removal of the rings by the birds themselves. Lovebirds, with their strong, clever beaks, are specialists in this—particularly when they were not banded until adult. Many birds will not eat or rest until the ring

has been removed and has disappeared somewhere in the sand or grit. This can lead to problems if the birds have already been registered in the official register which every [German] parrot breeder is required to keep and the bird is going to be put up for sale.

Bird shows are also social events between associations, but their main purpose is to increase the quality of breeding. All lovebirds behave quite well during those few days in their separate show cages if they have been accustomed to this since early youth through gradual isolation (after having been lured into the cage by means of some delicacy) and training in solitude, at first for hours, then for days.

Fischer's Lovebirds

Agapornis fischeri

The closest relatives of masked lovebirds are Fischer's lovebirds, which are only slightly smaller. Males and females have the same coloration.

The natural habitat of Fischer's lovebirds is northwest of that of the masked lovebirds, separated from it by jungle. They inhabit an area with a very similar ecological structure, although distinguished by slightly more cultivated land.

The voices of *A. fischeri* are louder and more strident than those of masked lovebirds. On the whole, Fischer's tend to be more lively. After the war, the numbers of *A. fischeri* were the fastest to recover, which shows the stamina of the birds. For many years, they were considered to be the best and most reliable breeders. Lately, their popularity suffered somewhat because their colors are not as bright and they do not show the same variety of color mutations as the other species. This is most likely due to the fact that they are not bred as often—but this may change tomorrow. In any case, their numbers in Europe are sufficient to assure a good supply at a reasonable price.

Fischer's lovebirds are very sociable and adaptable in the wild. There are accounts in Forshaw's book of their taking over abandoned weaver nests. Like masked lovebirds, they breed in colonies. Yellow and pied yellow *fischeri* have been bred in Germany for more than fifty years, with the yellow showing a pure, strong color except for the pale pink mask. Unfortunately, they were in the wrong hands. The breeders did not heed the advice of experts and did not breed the yellows with

The Fischer's lovebird is a lively bird with stamina.

Being a very sociable lovebird, yellow Fischer's adapt well. They have been known to take over abandoned weaver nests.

The albino Fischer's lovebird is extremely rare. Although the eye is red, it is only visible blood vessels and not coloration. The lovebird lacks any pigmentation whatsoever.

strong green birds; in order to multiply them quickly, they continued to interbreed them. Since the yellows were not strong and viable, they died out before becoming popular. Let this be a lesson to anyone fortunate enough to breed a new mutation (which is certainly within the realm of possibility with lovebirds). When a bird of a new color occurs, some inbreeding will be required because most mutations are recessive, probably requiring mating with a parent or a sibling to fix the new color. However, as soon as there is more than one bird of the new color, strong, vital, fertile natural-colored birds should be crossed with them to prevent the new mutation from dying out. Not by accident do scientists speak of a "loss mutation," in which there is not only a loss of color (lighter shades) but also a loss of other, at first less clearly apparent, qualities. If these negative qualities are doubled by inbreeding, a general loss of vitality and fertility will become noticeable, which may even lead to the death of the birds. All of today's apparently viable variations that are based on mutations have slowly and

patiently been bred for health and vitality by crossing with the best wild birds, which are the result of nature's own selection. In this manner, we have today once more quite pretty and easily bred

A beautiful yellow mutation of a Fischer's lovebird.

yellow and even more yellow-green *fischeri*. According to Rutgers (*Handbook of Foreign Birds,* 1969), there are reports of blues, yet according to the color composition of *A. fischeri,* they cannot be overly attractive as compared to the natural coloration. (See also blue *A. roseicollis*.)

In feeding and care Fischer's lovebirds have very similar requirements to those of masked lovebirds. They appear to be even slightly less susceptible to lower temperatures. However, the danger of frost damage to their feet remains and they too should winter in a frost-free area. Because Fischer's lovebirds have a greater tendency toward fighting than *A. personata*, they should be bred only by pairs in cages. However, breeding is encouraged when two pairs in adjacent cages are able to see and hear each other, even though they may fight occasionally through the bars. Sex determination is very difficult with this species, too. Young and resting birds may be put into frost-free aviaries without nesting boxes, like masked lovebirds.

Unfortunately, breeders and dealers have adopted the bad habit of referring to them as "Fischer's" for the sake of brevity, instead of using the pretty name "peach-headed." According to Hampe, the explorer Reichenow named this species in honor of Dr. G. A. Fischer, with whom he had discovered masked lovebirds and peach-heads on an exploratory voyage.

A recently imported group of Fischer's lovebirds.

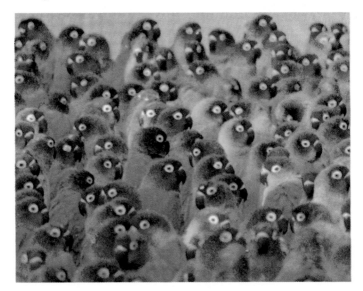

Fischer's lovebirds are found in northern Tanzania, southeast of Lake Victoria. Their natural habitat is the savannahs of the highlands at altitudes of 1000 to 1700 meters.

Nyasa Lovebirds

Agapornis lilianae

Nyasa, or Lilian's, lovebirds are the smallest of the species with white eye rings. They measure only four and one-half to five inches in length, and again, males and females are colored alike. Unfortunately, this smallest—one of the most beautiful, and up to now the rarest—eye-ring lovebird has remained in the hands of breeders since its breeding in

The lutino Nyasas are very bright yellow. They are small and somewhat delicate.

captivity in Europe has not been very successful. If we had not been able to obtain occasional imports of wild stock, this species might well have become extinct in our cages and aviaries.

According to Forshaw and Rutgers, their natural habitat is along the humid, wooded banks of the Zambesi River. Here they nest in knotholes of tall trees; they have also nested in the eaves of houses and in the abandoned nests of the buffalo weaver. As nesting materials, they use twigs, straw, and similar materials. They are not very selective in their choice of a nesting place or material. Without a doubt, the high temperatures and humidity in their natural breeding range work in their favor. They are said normally to lay four or five eggs. Breeders here have noticed a large incidence of infertile and dead-in-shell eggs and count themselves lucky to raise two fledglings from each clutch. The incubation period lasts for twenty-one days and begins with the laying of the first egg.

Outside the breeding season, *lilianae* often undertake more extensive group flights than their relatives, in flocks of a hundred birds or more, and they do no little damage to the millet fields. This is one reason why

Nyasa lovebirds, even though smaller than the masked, black-cheeked and Fischer's lovebirds, are dissatisfied with small cages. Since they are more peaceable than the other three species, they can be raised and bred in groups. De Grahl *(Papageien in Haus und Garten,* 1976) kept four pairs in a not overly large aviary. Under no circumstances should they be exposed to the

Even after breeding successes, the Nyasa remains the rarest of all the lovebirds with white eye rings.

winter temperatures of Europe, even though they do not require tropical heat.

In addition to the usual grains, they should be fed a lot of greens, fruits, berries, and sprouts. As nestling food, Pinter

45

Nyasa lovebird pairs are not aggressive toward other species of birds and can be kept in company with finches, weavers, budgerigars, cockatiels, doves and quails.

The male and female Nyasas are similar in color, but the red in the hen tends to be slightly paler.

(Handbuch der Papageienkunde, 1979) recommends bread moistened with milk—a good and simple food for many seed eaters. However, we must pay close attention to the absolute freshness of the food; sour milk will turn the best-intentioned feeding too easily into the opposite. Forshaw additionally mentions nectar from eucalyptus blossoms and the like as additional nutrition, so it will be no mistake if we offer the blossoms of fruit trees in spring.

In the U.S.A. there is already a strain of beautiful lutinos (pure yellow with red eyes and mask), but they have reached Europe only in negligible quantities. Pinter also mentions blue *lilianae*. Because of their similarity, breeders need to be cautioned against crossbreeding with *fischeri*. Young birds do not yet show the beautiful red of the head—this is a positive indication of youth. Finally, while Nyasa lovebirds are quite dainty, their voices are most definitely not!

Black-cheeked Lovebirds

Agapornis nigrigenis
These especially dainty African dwarf parrots (about five and one-half inches long) are particularly endangered in their pure form, both in the very small area of their range and in captivity, in spite of the fact that they are quite reliable breeders once they become used to their environment. Like the *lilianae* they live in the warm, humid climate of wooded river valleys. De Grahl mentions that temperatures of around 60

In the wild, black-cheeked lovebirds prefer to feed perched in trees or on grasses.

F. are indicated for fresh imports. They have been known to survive temperatures below freezing, he adds, and in captivity they breed up to three times in succession. The main danger to their survival in the wild, according to Forshaw, is excessive capture and exportation for the bird market. Thus we are called upon to care even more intensively for the purity of the remaining stock.

Many of the birds available for sale are not genetically pure. No other species of lovebird has had to suffer quite as much as the black-cheeked in regard to indiscriminate hybridization. The reasons are evident: their coloration and markings are apparently strongly dominant, they will readily breed with the masked lovebird, and they are much more expensive than the wild-colored masked lovebird. According to de Grahl, pure black-cheeked lovebirds must show no black head, no pure yellow on the throat, and no blue on the upper tail-coverts.

Their care and feeding are the same as for masked lovebirds. A large communal aviary and a colony breeding system of several pairs appear to

*A black-cheeked lovebird
normally colored.*

49

promise more success. *A. nigrigenis* shares this characteristic with *A. lilianae.* The size of the clutch is three to five eggs, and incubation lasts for twenty-four days. Naturally, from these two species some quite attractive hybrids have frequently been bred; these unfortunately turn into an unknown to date. The appearance of mutations always goes hand in hand with large numbers of domestically bred animals and is, therefore, a result of domestication. But first, more needs to be done for the preservation of the nice and easily kept and bred black-cheeked lovebird. Exhibition of

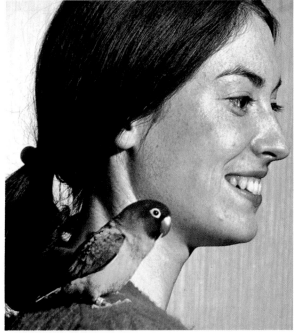

unattractive hodge-podge in succeeding generations, neither one nor the other. Since *A. lilianae* also are endangered, at least in Europe, such manipulations should evidently not be undertaken.

Color mutations of the black-cheeked are

The black-cheeked, as all lovebirds, are very tameable.

these birds should be undertaken for publicity purposes, because nothing attracts more attention to a good cause than the exhibition of healthy, domestically bred birds to the public.

All the white-eye-ring lovebirds, but particularly the larger, more robust masked and Fischer's are suited to liberty if the situation permits. Whoever lives in a single house surrounded by gardens may risk letting his breeding birds fly free from neighborhood, always returning to the feed dishes, even though many delicacies can be found outside. (Since buds, shoots, and fruit are favored tidbits, watch out for trouble with the neighbors!) From October, at the latest, through April

The beak of this black-cheeked lovebird is normal and not overgrown. Active birds usually keep their beaks trimmed.

the garden aviary. It is best to wait until there are babies in the nest, when the tie to the nest is strongest. When a trap door in the roof or upper third of the wire enclosure is opened, one or the other of the breeding pair will explore the surroundings but will not venture beyond calling distance of its mate's voice. Later, the fledglings will quickly and skillfully become accustomed to going in and out, and the entire flock will participate in excursions through the the door to the outside world should remain closed. If permitted constant liberty, lovebirds rarely leave the area, but they tend to build nests in the eaves of houses and similar places, revert to the wild, and eventually die in the frost and snow of winter.

Species Without White Eye Rings

The separation of lovebirds into species with and without white eye rings is not completely understandable. Rather, *A. roseicollis,* being closest to the species with eye rings,

The black-winged lovebird is one of five species without white eye rings.

represents a kind of link between them. Moreover, the species without eye rings are nowhere nearly as closely related among themselves as are those with eye rings, all of which are often considered subspecies of *A. personata.* The following five species can be clearly distinguished from one another by habitat, appearance, and behavior. However, they all share a rather peculiar and (for the observer) amusing manner of transporting nesting materials between the feathers on the back and rump, and occasionally on the chest. This is done mostly by the females, who take extraordinary, almost human, pains selecting and rejecting pieces of bark, loading themselves up, losing half of it, reloading, rising to the nesting hole heavily laden, losing half the cargo there, and starting over again. Somehow they manage to build a comfortable nest after all! This is one of their inborn traits which they cannot abandon even in captivity. Many bird lovers like to keep these little parrots mainly because of their amusing nesting habits, putting less value on breeding success. Unfortunately, this is quite irresponsible today, because with the exception of *A. roseicollis,* these species are endangered in Europe, and some even in their areas of origin.

Gray-headed lovebirds are among the species without white eye rings. The male is whitish gray on its upper body and the female is entirely green with a slightly brownish head.

Peach-faced Lovebirds

Agapornis roseicollis
This species, which inhabits a comparatively large area, is divided into two subspecies: *A. roseicollis* and, in southern Angola, the smaller, more intensely colored *A. r. catumbella*. Both are available in Europe through importation and are often unwittingly interbred. This renders almost insignificant the external sex characteristics cited by Hampe: The female: larger; wider base of beak; wider perching stance; smaller, rounder head; front paler red. The male: smaller; beak and perching stance narrower; larger, longer

A peach-faced lovebird.

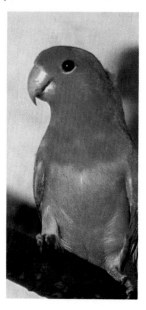

head; front brighter red. As with the four species with eye rings, the most accurate methods of sex determination here too are pelvic measurement and observation of behavior. When approached, the female disappears first into the box. Only females will tuck nesting materials between their feathers; young females will do this playfully even before reaching sexual maturity. It is almost exclusively the male that initiates courtship and regurgitates food from his crop.

Peach-faced lovebirds, which are bigger and stronger than the eye-ring species—and also louder—are considered the best adapted, most domesticated, and easiest-to-breed lovebirds. In their homeland, they live on steep, arid mountain cliffs on the edge of the desert. Here they breed in colonies in rock caves, on buildings, and in abandoned nests of social weavers and stripe-breasted sparrow-weavers. To gather food and drink they undertake long flights daily. In Africa, the breeding period coincides with the rainy season (January to March). At that time, the flocks are only small; outside of the

breeding season, however, *roseicollis* may gather by the hundreds and cause considerable damage to crops.

The first peach-faced lovebirds came to Germany in 1860 and were successfully bred there in 1869. They lay three to five

Today, the peach-faced lovebird are the most commonly kept and most numerous of all the lovebirds. Shown above is subspecies Agapornis roseicollis catumbella.

eggs, occasionally six. Incubation lasts from twenty-one to twenty-three

The attractive yellow in the creamino (albino) peach-faced lovebird is produced when yellow and blue are crossed.

days, nestling time five to six weeks; after another two weeks, the young are on their own. The juvenile plumage resembles that of adults, but all the colors are paler. Because of a tendency towards quarreling among peach-faces, and even more so toward other birds, it was believed for a long time that they should be kept and bred by pairs only. Among breeders today cages at least thirty-two inches are considered the minimum. It is possible, however, to breed several pairs of *roseicollis* in a spacious aviary. If the flights are particularly large, the growing young birds can remain there. When pairs are bred separately in breeding cages, to prevent injuries inflicted by the parent birds the fledglings should be removed as soon as they are self-sufficient.

Care and feeding are similar to those of the species with eye rings. We should offer more and larger sunflower seeds, as well as dry or germinated oats and wheat. If we also offer plenty of greens and fruit, a special breeding diet should not be necessary. Many pairs may not even accept it. Young birds are more likely to try out a new diet.

The whiteface blue peach-faced lovebird is not actually the purest of blue, but turquoise or pale yellowish-green.

When breeding there occasionally may be difficulties due to the often over-developed nest-building instinct of the species, which may lead to the building of a new nest on top of one in which eggs have already been laid or to abandoning a clutch in favor of beginning the construction of a new nest in another box. Once we become aware of this, spare nesting boxes must be removed after a maximum of three clutches or the pairs must be

A peach-faced lovebird of wild-colored, or normal, coloration.

separated; otherwise, they will continue to breed, which will weaken the female, often leading to her death. In addition, weakened *roseicollis* females easily become egg bound, which is often noticed only when it is too late to save them.

The eyes of the cinnamon peach-faced lovebird darken as it grows older.

The pink down covering of the newly hatched babies is another indication of the close relationship with the eye-ring species. Peach-faced lovebirds have repeatedly been crossed with masked and Fischer's lovebirds; the offspring exhibited the markings of the *A. roseicollis* but were, as far as they were tested, not fertile.

In the first decades of breeding peach-faced lovebirds, there was a lamentably high incidence of embryos dead in their shells shortly before hatching. This was ascribed to a lack of humidity in the air. Many methods were used to try and improve that situation, from misting the boxes to positioning containers with moss and sponges below the nests. Since the birds in their homeland nest in very arid areas (at best only the use of rotting nesting materials could possibly increase the humidity within the nest), lack of humidity could not be the only reason for the embryonic deaths. This suspicion has been corroborated by the birds themselves in terms of their adaptation to the European climate. The incidence of unhatched embryos has dropped so drastically that the problem of humidity is rarely discussed any longer. Still, a bone-dry attic room is not suited for

A bath should be given early in the day to allow plenty of time for the feathers to dry.

The yellow (cherry-head) peach-faced lovebird.

the breeding of lovebirds, and care should be taken that the humidity does not go lower than 65%. When, in addition, we see to the availability of fresh willow twigs during the breeding season (de Grahl recommends also lime and birch), this source of danger can be virtually eliminated. Diminishing fertility as a consequence of domestication and occasionally inbreeding is another matter.

Peach-faced Lovebird

In breeding for color mutations, the peach-faced lovebird is second only to the budgerigar in rapid development of divergent colors. This is to be taken literally because today, with only very few exceptions, all the mutations known from the budgerigar can be found in the plumage of the peach-faced lovebird. (In the author's budgerigar books the coloration of the plumage, and its development, structure,

The blue peach-faced lovebird has become the most common mutation.

and inheritance are treated: *Budgerigars* and *Encyclopedia of Budgerigars,* T.F.H. Publications.)

According to de Grahl, a blue peach-faced lovebird was observed in the wild. In captivity, though, the first mutation (in the fifties) was the dominant pied yellow-green birds. As with a majority of pied variations, this trait can only be called partly dominant. At first, only birds with lighter, flecked heads appeared. When they were paired with each other, their offspring showed a wide pattern variation, with no two birds resembling one another, and the color ranging from predominantly green to predominantly yellow. Today, the pied birds can be considered thoroughly established. The international exhibition standard prefers pied peach-faces marked 50:50, with mostly symmetrical markings. These birds have kept the peach mask, which should be pure, as should the blue rump, which is merely shaded toward turquoise. This latter characteristic differentiates the pied birds from the true yellow (in place of which dilute pied birds are occasionally

and fraudulently offered for sale).

Many pied green-yellow birds tend to show red-flecked feathers elsewhere than on the mask, but these birds have not shown themselves to be an inheritable modification (de Grahl). Many breeders tend to consider this coloration as an indication of some deficiency, since it often appears in older birds or disappears again at the next molt.

One of the most

Homemade nest boxes are always welcomed by lovebirds.

attractive color mutations of *A. roseicollis* is the "Golden Cherry" bred by the Japanese in the late fifties. It shows red and blue on a golden yellow ground with the same intensity as that of wild birds. The blue is merely a little paler, the yellow with a faint greenish tinge. The first *roseicollis* of this variety were exported to Switzerland at a high price. Offspring later came to Holland and Germany. Comparatively good success in breeding has led to somewhat lowered prices, but these birds are still in great demand. The name "Golden Cherry" has been kept in other languages for lack of something better. A little later, the Americans bred a similar mutant which they called (according to Ochs) the "Imperial Cherryhead." It is characteristic of the Swiss sense of simple democracy that these birds are simply called "yellow-greens" there. One authority accurately calls them "bordered" or "scaled." Indeed, the greenish yellow plumage of these birds show almost a

ghost image outlining the feathers, similar to that of many thinned-down budgie colorations; the large feathers are pale gray, the rump thinned-down blue. The ground color varies from almost yellow to almost green.

Pretty as a picture are the lutino peach-faced lovebirds, which are pure yellow with the exception of the red mask and eyes. All horny parts are of a pale flesh color in this sex-linked mutation. It is recommended that lutinos be crossed with strong, wild-colored greens to keep them strong and to maintain their coloration.

Cinnamon and dilute varieties have already been bred from *roseicollis*. They have paler colors, lighter horny parts, and brownish wings as characteristics distinguishing them from the wild coloration. Both have reddish eyes as nestlings, but while those of the cinnamon variety

Sunflower seeds are enjoyed by most lovebirds.

TROPICAL FISH HOBBYIST

Helping marine, freshwater, and herptile hobbyists for 42 years

Temperate Marine Fishes

The Paludarium: A New Challenge

Since 1952, *Tropical Fish Hobbyist* has been the source of accurate, up-to-the-minute, and fascinating information on every facet of the aquarium hobby. Join the more than 50,000 devoted readers worldwide who wouldn't miss a single issue.

Subscribe right now so you don't miss a single copy!

Return To:

Tropical Fish Hobbyist, P.O. Box 427, Neptune, NJ 07753-0427

YES! Please enter my subscription to *Tropical Fish Hobbyist*. Payment for the length I've selected is enclosed. U.S. funds only.

CHECK ☐ 1 year-$30   ☐ 2 years-$55   ☐ 3 years-$75   ☐ 5 years-$120
ONE: 12 ISSUES   24 ISSUES   36 ISSUES   60 ISSUES

(Please allow 4-6 weeks for your subscription to start.) *Prices subject to change without notice*

☐ LIFETIME SUBSCRIPTION (max 30 Years) $495
☐ SAMPLE ISSUE $3.50
☐ GIFT SUBSCRIPTION. Please send a card announcing this gift. I would like the card to read: _____
☐ I don't want to subscribe right now, but I'd like to have one of your FREE catalogs listing books about pets. Please send catalog to:

SHIP TO:

Name _____

Street _____ Apt. No. _____

City _____ State _____ Zip _____

U.S. Funds Only. Canada add $11.00 per year; Foreign add $16.00 per year.

Charge my: ☐ VISA   ☐ MASTER CHARGE   ☐ PAYMENT ENCLOSED

Card Number _____ Expiration Date _____

Cardholder's Name (if different from "Ship to":) _____

Cardholder's Address (if different from "Ship to":) _____

Cardholder's Signature _____

T.F.H. Publications publishes more than 1000 books covering many hobby aspects (dogs, cats, birds, fish, small animals, etc.). Whether you are a beginner or an advance hobbyist you will find exactly what you're looking for among our complete listing of books. For a free catalog fill out the form on the other side of this page and mail it tod

. . CATS . . .

. . . BIRDS . .

. . . REPTILES . . .

. . . DOGS . . .

THE WORLD'S LARGEST SELECTION OF PET BOOKS.

. . FISH . . .

darken as they grow older, those of the dilutes remain reddish for life.

Much more importance must be ascribed to the blue series. As is the case with budgerigars, it is possible to speak of distinct blue and green series in *A. roseicollis.* As evidenced by the color photographs, the blue peach-faced lovebirds are not really blue, as are blue masked lovebirds, but turquoise or pale yellowish green. So far, the yellow pigment has not been completely removed from *A. roseicollis.* It is merely changed, thinned-down, so to speak, which is equally true of the rose red that remains noticeable on the front of the blues and has not quite disappeared from the delicate gray of their neck feathers.
Consequently, pied blue

This peach-faced lovebird has sought out the highest perch available, which is common practice for all lovebirds.

birds, which were easily bred through greens in two generations, are not blue-white, but pied blue-yellow (blue is recessive to green, as in budgerigars). Their coloration strongly resembles that of the pied forms of yellow-faced blue budgies and they are called just that by many breeders. It is assumed that most breeders of lovebirds are familiar with the blues for color inheritance in the budgerigar, because the topic of color breeding understandably exceeds the scope of a book dealing only with the species of lovebirds. One authority recommends crossing pied greens with blues, for the enhancement of their coloration. This applies not

Wide variations are possible in peach-faced mutations.

only for pieds but also for all greens and blues, because it has become a "golden rule" in breeding budgerigars for more than a hundred years: green enhances blue, and vice versa.

Lutinos had to be bred with blues to obtain albinos, which also have a sex-linked inheritance. These are presently available, but because of the incomplete removal of the yellow pigment they cannot be pure white. Rather they are a pale lemon yellow and therefore quite attractive. There are also bordered, cinnamon, and dilute birds from the blue strain in this pale yellow ground color, the creation of which is not difficult if the rules of color selection in budgerigars are followed.

We know also that all color strains of *A. roseicollis* are ruled by the presence or absence of so-called dark factors (Bielfeld, *Handbook of Lovebirds,* T.F.H. Publications). The wild-colored *roseicollis* has no dark factor and is therefore on the same level as the light-green budgerigar. The dark-green *roseicollis* has one dark factor and appears noticeably darker (jade) green, with an ultramarine-colored rump. The olive variety, with two dark factors, is of a dull olive color with a dark blue-gray rump, which resembles the shade of the mauve budgerigar. Wild-colored birds (light green without a dark factor) are homozygous, as are the olive variety. Paired among series: the common turquoise-colored "light blue" without a dark factor; the only slightly darker colored "dark blue" (its rump color like that of the dark green) with one dark factor; and the "mauve" (as in the budgerigar) with two dark factors. This bird is lead-

themselves, olives will produce offspring that look like their parents because there can be no more than two factors. Dark greens, however, with one dark factor, are of intermediate inheritance, and their offspring will be divided into 25% light green (wild-colored), 25% olive, and 50% dark green. The same holds true in the blue

Dark markings on the bills of young peach-faced lovebirds is characteristic.

colored on its upper side, light gray on the underside, with the mask faintly red. The gray has a very faint red tinge throughout, so that mauve is the absolutely correct name for this coloration.

Inheritance is the same as for the different color shades of the greens. As blue factors are recessive to green, all greens split to blue interact with blue according to the presence, absence, or double presence of the dark

When approached, the female peach-faced lovebird will go into the nest box first.

factor. Here are some examples—the color after the slash (/) indicates the recessive color: (1) Light-green x light-blue = 100% light-green/blue. (2) Light-green/blue x light-green/blue = 50% light-green/blue,25% light-green (homozygous), 25% light-blue. (3) Light-green/blue x light-blue = 50% light-green/blue, 50% light-blue. (4) Dark-green/blue x light-blue = 25% light-green/blue, 25% dark-green/blue, 25% light-blue, 25% light-blue, 25% dark-blue. (5) Olive/blue x light-blue = 50% dark-green/blue, 50% dark-blue. (6) Dark-green/blue x dark-blue = light-green/blue, dark-green/blue, olive/blue, light-blue, dark-blue, mauve. (7) Olive/blue x dark-blue = as above, but proportionately more olive/blue and mauve. (8) Olive/blue x mauve = 50% olive/blue, 50% mauve, (since both have two dark factors).

Simpler: (1) Light-green x light-green = 100% light-green. (2) Olive x olive = 100% olive. (3) Mauve x mauve = 100% mauve.

But: (1) Dark-green x dark-green = 25% light-green, 25% olive, 50% dark-green. (2) Dark-blue x dark-blue = 25% light-blue, 25% mauve, 50% dark-blue.

Of course, the percentages indicated are accurate only with 100 young, and the results may differ from brood to brood. The cited examples can only indicate what to expect from a given pairing. In all these examples the inheritance is not sex linked.

Even though peach-faced lovebirds with one or two dark factors may not be as striking in color as the comparable budgerigars, their important role in the breeding of distinctively marked pied mutations that are rich in contrast should not be overlooked, nor should that of the greens for the enhancement of the color of all yellows. Grays are just one step removed from gray-greens through ordinary greens, as in budgerigars. The gray is said to be a muddy gray-blue, with a lighter underside. Gray-winged birds and birds with lighter coloring above and darker underside are said to exist, results of dark-green/blue x dark-green/blue, which show two shades of blue in their plumage. It is not unlikely that the breeding of *A. roseicollis* still has many surprises in store—one more reason to warn against careless, uninformed experiments.

As long as other circumstances are of no significance, peach-faced lovebirds are particularly suited to liberty. In the bird park at the Hermann Monument in the Teutoburg Forest, an entire flock comes and goes as it pleases, even nesting under the eaves of neighboring frame houses. Its owner had previously gained experience with them in his own garden. They are a sight to be seen!

A peach-faced lovebird with dark factors that do darken the plumage.

Red-faced Lovebird

Agapornis pullaria

This particularly colorful and lively little parrot has been Problem Bird No. 1 among lovebirds. The main reason is probably a lack of adaptability as far as its choice of a nesting site is concerned. Even though the species was discovered in the seventeenth century and imported soon after, and while much printer's ink has been used up in writing about these birds, there is insufficient or even contradictory information in the relevant literature.

The song of a red-faced lovebird is a pleasant chirping.

The description of size alone varies from five inches (Rutgers) to five and one-half (de Grahl) to six inches (Pinter). Even in Forshaw's work, otherwise considered scientifically accurate, there is only vague information concerning their activities in the wild, and the information referring to breeding habits is based on the observation of captive birds.

A. pullaria shows a wide distribution, living mainly on flat grassy steppes and the edges of light forestation. Grass seeds are their main staple, but berries and fruit, particularly wild figs, are also eaten. To the regret of the human population, red-faced lovebirds often devour entire millet fields; they know how to climb the stalks and how to descend head first!

As a nesting site, they prefer termite mounds, in which the walls consist of leaves which the termites glued together into a rigid cork-like mass. Into this, the females alone (the males participate only by courtship singing) dig a tunnel, which ends in a fist-sized hollow. For nesting material they collect only leaves and small pieces of bark. No tube- or bowl-

This red-faced male lovebird exhibits the characteristics of the species. Note the blue carpal edge on the wing and the red area in the tail.

shaped nest is built, as with the previously cited species. The size of the clutch varies from two to seven eggs. The female alone incubates them for about twenty-two days. The young are covered with gray down. After four to six weeks, they leave the nest. In juvenile plumage the males can be distinguished by the black undersides of their wings (green in females). The red face mask is yellowish in the young of both sexes. In their mature plumages, the males and females of red-faced lovebirds are easily

The red-faced lovebird is an excellent climber and will even descend head first. This is the subspecies pullaria.

distinguished, because the females are slightly paler in all their colors. In Uganda there is a subspecies that differs slightly in color (paler) and size (larger): *A. p. ugandae.*

Hampe has mentioned the endurance and lack of susceptibility to cold of the species kept in northern latitudes, once the birds have been carefully acclimated; all other

and mealworm larvae should be given (hemp and sunflower seeds are rarely accepted). Rutgers complains that red-faced lovebirds will often eat only millet. Unfortunately, this matter may become insignificant because red-faced lovebirds are rarely

These red-faced lovebird chicks are thirty days old and still developing their normal colors.

authorities emphasize a need for warmth and the general delicateness of the species in captivity. Even in regard to their diet, the information of the various authors differs considerably: Hampe and Pinter refer to a varied diet: in addition to a good exotic mixture, fruit, ant eggs,

obtainable commercially. Though comparatively inexpensive and frequently available after the last war, this species is absent from the market at present. It is possible, however, that this is due to a lack of demand. The word has spread that *A. pullaria* are not as easily kept and simply cannot be bred sufficiently under human care. Thus it would certainly be irresponsible to increase the number of birds taken from their already endangered environment. This is very unfortunate for the bird lover, because red-faced lovebirds are charming companions, lovable and lively in manner, quite tame with patient training, and—above all—not as raucous as their (probably not very close) relatives. Their song is pleasant chirping, their plumage colorful, and the sexes are easily distinguishable.

If any of our readers should still own red-faced lovebirds, or if the species should once more become available in the trade, it will be helpful to have the few known facts about successful and attempted breedings in captivity.

The red of the face, the black of the eyes, and the green of the body make the red-faced lovebird a bird of contrast and beauty.

The subspecies ugandae *of the red-faced lovebird differs slightly in color and is larger in size than* pullaria.

Around 1900, a successful attempt was made in Germany in an ordinary nesting box, but further details are not available. Hampe mentions a pair which in 1937 fed each other, mated repeatedly, and attempted to dig a tunnel into the stucco wall of their aviary after ignoring ordinary nesting boxes and a special concrete hole. The female persisted in loosening the mortar in one place until finally, with the help of the breeder, a sufficiently large cavity was formed. In it, the female built a nest of willow twigs, which she carried in her feathers. She laid and incubated five eggs, which were either not fertilized or contained dead embryos. In 1957, limited success was attained in England and by Hampe in Germany. In England, peat moss had been stuffed into hanging barrels and nesting cavities scooped out. Almost all of the fifteen pairs in this specially equipped aviary bred, but only one healthy youngster survived. In Germany, Hampe took the trouble of erecting a clay wall, into which a female dug a cavity by herself. One young bird hatched but did not survive. In Capetown, successful attempts involved very large aviaries containing only single pairs. The installations included large nest boxes filled with cork blocks and hung in tree branches. Two-inch holes were bored into the cork (de Grahl; no further information). In

The male red-faced lovebird must accompany the female when she begins to dig a nest. This action triggers the breeding instinct.

The red-faced lovebird is difficult to breed in captivity due to the bird's lack of adaptability with respect to nesting sites.

Switzerland, there was finally one successful breeding after four years of failure with the same pair (de Grahl).

When comparing and evaluating these facts, so widely separated in time and space, one thing becomes evident: the female needs to dig her own nest into porous but not-too-loose material, in the company of a male ready for mating. Only this will trigger their breeding instinct. The low incidence of hatching and the high mortality of the babies may well be caused by lack of experience. If there were more breeding attempts and more red-faced lovebirds in the possession of breeders, it would be possible to discover the elements lacking in their diet and care. In the absence of nest boxes, red-faced lovebirds have been said to occasionally sleep hanging upside down in the manner of hanging parrots *(Loriculus* species).

Abyssinian Lovebirds

Agapornis taranta
This largest species of lovebird (six and one-half inches) is at home in the wild mountains of Ethiopia, to an altitude of 9,000 feet. For this reason, they readily survive our winters in outdoor aviaries with an attached, unheated shelter room. One requirement, of course, is careful acclimation. The difference in altitude may cause more problems for the birds than the change of temperature.

The Abyssinian lovebird has also been referred to as the black-winged lovebird.

Hampe cites an instance of a pair kept at liberty which began to breed in November at a temperature of around 40 F. In a starling box they hatched four healthy youngsters in mid winter at temperatures of about 25 F. It goes without saying that this should remain an exception, and winter breeding should be avoided if possible.

The natural habitat of Abyssinian, or black-winged, lovebirds lies along the edges of evergreen mountain forests of the Abyssinian plateau, from where they descend, according to Forshaw, only when the figs are ripe, in small groups of up to ten birds. Despite a short fleeing distance, they rarely approach human habitations. This species nests separately, not in colonies, in hollow trees and knotholes. It does not appear to have a clearly defined breeding season. The females carry twigs and bark as nesting material, usually between the feathers of the chest and rump, but occasionally in their beaks. They simply put down a layer of these materials in a hollow, into which they lay three to five eggs, rarely six. The female incubates alone for twenty-four to twenty-five days, during which she is fed by the male. The hatchlings are covered with white fuzz, which later changes to gray. They leave the nest at six to eight weeks and

Abyssinian lovebirds. The male is identified by the red coloration around the eyes and forehead.

immediately fly quite well; nevertheless, the male continues to feed them for a few more weeks. There are no data available on successive breedings, if any. Their diet consists of several grass and tree seeds and fruit, although they are said to particularly enjoy bitter juniper berries.

The first Abyssinian lovebirds were imported to Austria in 1906, with a first breeding success in Vienna in 1911. In 1923, they were imported to

Abyssinian Lovebird

England and from there in larger numbers to Germany. According to Pinter, some imported birds proceeded to breed successfully after only eight months. Altogether, this species cannot be considered easy to breed successfully, and it has never been very popular, despite many endearing

Female Abyssinian. The green of the hen is less vibrant then that of the male.

qualities (it probably was never widely available on the market, either). It is possible that only the larger form *A. t. taranta* was imported, because there is no mention of the much smaller *A. t. nana* in the cited reports on care and breeding.

Some of the positive qualities of the Abyssinian lovebird have just been mentioned. To these must be added the fact of easy sex determination after the very first feathers have grown. The young males have wings black on the underside, while in the same place the females first are greenish, later gray black. Many male fledglings already show the red eye rings, and the first red feathers on the head begin to sprout a little later, even though full coloration is not reached until about nine months of age. The birds are quiet and almost modest, uttering only an occasional soft chirping.

Their diet should be similar to that of the species with eye rings, with perhaps more sunflower seeds, only they need not be the white or striped kind. With their strong beaks, the Abyssinian lovebirds manage to open even the cheaper, black kind. They prefer fruit, such as apples and pears, to greens, but should be offered both. They also enjoy eating the bark of willow twigs; in winter, figs are the greatest delicacy.

Even though they are not susceptible to cold, summer is the best breeding time because of the availability of sun, greens, and fruit. Abyssinian lovebirds need slightly larger nesting boxes, which according to Rutgers should measure 11 x 4 x 12 inches high. It is best to place an inch and a half of peat moss or coarse sawdust and wood shavings into the boxes, since not all females collect nesting materials. For this reason also, the floor should have a slight hollow. It is nevertheless recommended to have available moss, dry leaves of nonpoisonous trees, and tree bark for those females who wish to construct a nest, according to Rutgers. Pinter mentions that some females do construct even quite elaborate nests.

Hand-raised Abyssinians become exceptionally tame and affectionate. I once saw a male who rode through the entire house and out onto the terrace on his owner's shoulder without leaving her.

The greatest drawback of these pleasant birds is their quarrelsomeness. Their quiet demeanor is misleading; they suddenly attack another bird's legs and will not let go, so that they often kill smaller birds and seriously injure larger ones. Unfortunately, this can also happen at the mesh separating flights. For this reason, a double wall of wire mesh at a distance of a couple of inches is recommended. We must strictly enforce the keeping of only one

A male Abyssinian. Adult coloration is reached by nine months of age.

pair per flight. Only parakeets larger than crimson rosellas, whom they cannot hurt, may be used as companions, one pair of each. Even cockatiels and red-rumped parrots have had their legs

bitten, according to de Grahl. Because of the unpredictable behavior of the Abyssinians, their own young should be removed as soon as they are self-sufficient.

Unfortunately, Abyssinians have a more pronounced proclivity for feather plucking than any of the other lovebirds, whether their own or those of other birds, and even the down of their nestlings, which may lead to torn skin and death. One authority recommends giving the birds diatomaceous earth combined with vitamins to prevent further plucking as a result of some deficiency. Otherwise, the picked-on youngsters will have to be put into a separate cage within the parents' flight, so that the adults will have to feed them through the wire,

Facing page: With the black of the underwing in full view, this male Abyssinian takes flight. Below: Abyssinian lovebirds are quiet and modest, and will only utter a soft chirp.

which they will usually do quite readily. Of course, the young must have reached about the age where they can survive on their own, because otherwise they will catch cold too easily.

Hampe succeeded in having Abyssinian babies raised by budgerigars, although only as long as they were in the nest, and after the young budgies were removed. After fledging, however, they were no longer fed by the budgerigars; until they were self-sufficient they had to be fed a gruel by means of a feeding syringe.

Black-collared Lovebirds

Agapornis swinderniana
The natural range of black-collared lovebirds is so large that three geographic races are distinguished, yet less is known about them than about any other lovebirds. According to the literature, these lovebirds have never been brought to Europe and were caged,

This mounted specimen of a black-collared lovebird shows the well-defined black collar.

unsuccessfully, only once, in the Congo. There, they would only eat fig seeds, and only if offered in whole fresh figs. Yet an analysis of their stomach contents shows that these birds eat other fruits as well, and also millet, half-ripe corn, insect larvae, and caterpillars. Theoretically, it should be possible with modern nutritional science to hand-feed them with a nourishing, protein-rich diet by means of a feeding syringe put directly into the crop until they are willing to accept germinated Senegal millet or similar small seeds.

Unfortunately, there are no black-collared lovebirds available on the market. My personal friend and noted German lovebird breeder, Siegfried Bischoff, on his own initiative undertook an expedition in 1979 to their homeland to find out more about them. He only saw—and even that is not quite certain—several birds fly by at a distance. Therefore, we can only reproduce a picture, not a color photograph. Yet black-collared lovebirds have been known since 1820, according to Hampe. They measure five to six inches and are the only species whose habitat is the dense tropical forest, to an altitude of about 6,000 feet. From there, small flocks of fifteen to twenty birds are said to make excursions to neighboring grain fields, but mostly they remain in the dense forest canopy, rarely descending to the ground.

The nominate subspecies of the black-collared lovebird.

As mentioned previously, their preferred food seems to be fresh fig seeds, which they pick from the ripe fruit; yet even in the fertile tropical climate, these are not available the year round, which leads us to believe that the birds must eat other things too.

It is quite possible that black-collared lovebirds are often overlooked because of their soft coloring and soft voices. Therefore, the estimates concerning their numbers are very vague, and observations of breeding habits are practically nonexistent. Neither nests nor eggs have been described. It can only be assumed that they breed in tree cavities in July, since males with fully developed gonads were captured in July, according to Forshaw. Thus, these birds offer an exciting challenge to explorers!

According to Hampe, the *A. s. zenkeri* differs from *A. s. swinderniana* by a wide orange-to-red-brown neckband. Their range is the former Cameroons. *A. s. emini* is larger, with a coarser, hooked beak. They occur in the central Congo and western Uganda, isolated from *A. s. zenkeri* geographically.

As forest dwellers, black-collared lovebirds spend most of their time in the tree-tops. Shown below is the subspecies Agapornis swinderniana zenkeri.

Perhaps it will be possible one day to capture and import these elusive birds and to get to know them after successful importation and acclimation. Until then, lovebird fanciers have the happy task of caring for all the other *Agapornis* species in order to preserve them for future generations, independent of further importation. This

The preferred food of the black-collared lovebird is fig seeds. Shown above is the subspecies Agapornis swinderniana emini.

is particularly true of the many species which are presently endangered: *A. nigrigenis, A. lilianae, A. taranta*, and, above all, *A. pullaria*, whose domestic numbers have shrunk alarmingly.

Gray-headed Lovebirds

Agapornis cana

As different as they may appear at first sight, these little island inhabitants only five inches long are the closest relatives of *A. taranta,* mentioned previously. When observed closely, a visible similarity is found in the darkness of the tips of the tail feathers in both species. More similarities are shown in their behavior. Both breed separately in hollow trees, and both usually carry their sparse nesting materials of dried or evergreen leaves

The natural range of the gray-headed lovebird is confined to the island of Madagascar and its neighboring islands.

tucked between the feathers on the rump. In the pertinent literature, both species are said to occasionally build elaborate nests in the manner of the lovebirds with eye rings. In both species, male and females remain faithfully together and except for the breeding season band

together with others in small-to-medium-sized flocks. In captivity, they remain quite shy and will always be unpleasant and aggressive towards other species of birds.

Gray-headed lovebirds, found on the island of Madagascar and its neighbors, appear in two geographically isolated subspecies. In the southwest of Madagascar, the species *A. c. ablectanea* occurs. It is distinguished from *A. c. cana* by a more bluish hue to its plumage, with the males showing a purer and more extensive gray.

Outside of the breeding season these birds often roam about in flocks of varying sizes, doing considerable damage to the rice fields. They are noisy and lively but would rather not cross large open areas. They like to rest huddled closely together in date palms along the way. Their flight is undulating, not straight-line, as that of the other species of lovebirds. Their fleeing distance is considerable; that is, they are quite shy, even in the wild. Grass seeds, their main staple, are picked from the ground, where the birds walk about with rapid movements. They are said to associate on their foraging trips with finches of the genera *Lonchura* or *Foudia*. On some of the smaller islands off the east coast of Africa, as well as on the coast, *A. cana* are said to have been introduced but have died out (Forshaw). Other islands they colonized by themselves and can still be found there.

The usual number of eggs in a clutch is three or four, occasionally as many as seven. Incubation lasts for eighteen to twenty-two days. The young leave the nest at five to six weeks, fully feathered. In the wild the young males are said

Not suited for everyone, gray-headed lovebirds require love, patience, and suitable accommodations. Shown below is the subspecies Agapornis cana ablectanea.

to be pure green when they leave the nest and indistinguishable from the females; in captivity, they clearly show the gray head and neck, even though somewhat diluted. Similar instances of bypassing the juvenile plumage in captivity are known in other species of birds, but as yet there are no plausible explanations for this phenomenon. Young

A gray-headed lovebird cock.

gray-heads attain their full adult coloration at four to five months.

Today their exportation from Madagascar is prohibited. Consequently, it is a considerable success that domestically bred gray-headed lovebirds are once again exhibited at all major shows. It is doubtful, however, whether the present domestic stock is sufficient to ensure the future of the species in captivity.

While imported gray-heads need to be kept warm in a heated environment in the winter, at least until acclimated, those bred in captivity are hardier and can withstand colder temperatures, but they must be protected from frost and damp drafts. Since the gray-heads do not get along with each other and the females especially fight over nesting boxes, each pair should have its own small aviary, if possible. A particularly peaceable and close pair, though, can often share a bigger aviary with peaceable species of large parakeets.

As soon as gray-heads are able to maintain their fleeing distance, they become more pleasant and can be bred successfully. Roomy budgerigar nest boxes are preferred, with a layer of sawdust or peat moss. The birds are not choosy about nesting material, but they tend to amass empty millet sprays. Gray-heads have an interesting courtship behavior. The males dance around the females, which often hang upside down from nesting boxes to indicate their readiness to breed; this makes perches a necessity.

Many parents resent inspection of the nest box. In order to band the babies, it is recommended that the parents be enticed from the nest box by means of some favorite tidbit. When banding, the rings should be pushed over the front toes to the joint, and the back toe pulled gently through the ring by means of a flattened stick. The best time for banding is usually on about the twelfth day, but experience will be the best teacher, from case to case and species to species.

Dry (even better, germinated) spray millet is their favorite delicacy. Their diet should be the same as that for other small lovebirds. Since not all gray-heads like greens, they should become accustomed quite early to a conditioning food that includes grated carrots.

It is possible to keep these species at liberty during the summer, if the partners have first become used to flying in and out singly. De Grahl says that domestically bred gray-heads showed no discomfort at 16 F., but such experiments are not recommended with this species, as it is quite rare today. These birds cannot survive a winter in the open.

A hand-raised youngster even learned to repeat a few words, according to Hampe. Gray-headed

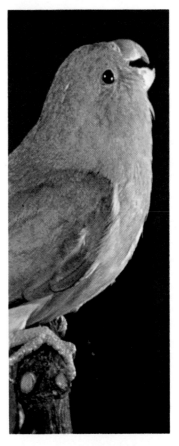

The female gray-headed lovebird lacks the gray head that is found on the male.

lovebirds which will be exhibited should be trained to the show cages carefully from earliest youth, since otherwise they tend to fuss loudly and assume stiff and unnatural poses.

PARROTS AND RELATED BIRDS by Henry Bates and Robert Busenbark (H-912)

This is the "bible" for parrot lovers. It has more color photographs and more information on parrot keeping than any other single book on the subject. Chapters on parrots in aviculture, feeding, housing, taming, talking, breeding, and hand-rearing are followed by sections on the various groups and particular species.

Illustrated with 107 black-and-white and 160 color photos. Hard cover, 5½ × 8½", 543 pp.

HANDBOOK OF LOVEBIRDS by Horst Bielfeld (H-1040)

Thorough coverage of the genus *Agapornis* is the principal feature of this work: a description of life in the wild is amplified by chapters on care and breeding in captivity. The species accounts cover all of the lovebird forms. Fanciers of the many lovebird color varieties will appreciate the extensive and authoritative gallery of photographs and the inheritance tables that summarize the genetic principles involved. Included is a lengthy section on diseases of parrots, by Dr. Manfred Heidenreich, which surveys the various illnesses common to all parrot species.

Illustrated with 117 color and 10 black-and-white photos. Hard cover, 8½ × 11", 109 pp.

PARROTS OF THE WORLD by Joseph M. Forshaw (PS-753)

Every species and subspecies of parrot in the world, including those recently extinct, is covered in this authoritative work. Almost 500 species or subspecies appear in the color illustrations by William T. Cooper. Descriptions are accompanied by distribution maps and accounts of behavior, feeding habits, and nesting.

Almost 300 color plates. Hard cover, 9½ × 12½", 584 pp.

Index

Page numbers in parentheses refer to illustrations.

Abyssinian lovebird, 78-83; (9, 78–83)
African savannah, 9
Aggression, 42, 57, 81, 88, 90
Atavism, 16

Banding, 35, 37, 91; (35)
Black-cheeked lovebird, 48-51; (9, 10, 48–51)
Black-collared lovebird, 84–87, (84–87)
Blue varieties, 33, 47, 63–69
Bordered varieties, 63–66
Breeding behavior, 9–11, 16–17, 26, 33, 38–41, 44, 48–50, 54, 58–59, 63–68, 70, 74–78
Budgerigar (parakeet), 34, 62, 64–69, 83

Cinnamon varieties, 64–65
Color varieties, 16, 34, 41, 50, 62, 63–68

Dark factor, 68
Dark green varieties, 65–69
Diatomaceous earth, 83
Dilute varieties, 64–66
Double-wiring, 83

Egg binding, 59
Eggs, 9, 30, 44, 58, 72, 78, 89
Exhibiting, 35, 50

Feather-plucking, 82
Feeding, 10, 27–28, 42, 45–46, 48, 57, 70, 73, 80, 84, 91
Fischer's lovebird, 38–42, (13, 38–41)

Golden Cherry mutation, 63
Gray-headed lovebird, 88–91, (9, 88–91)

Hand-raising, 22, 25, 83–84, 91
Houseplants, poisonous, 22
Housing, 18, 26–28, 42, 45, 48, 56, 75, 78, 82, 90, (20, 22, 26, 31, 32)
Humidity, 60

Hybrids, 16–17, 34, 48
Incubation, 9, 30, 44, 55, 72, 78, 89, (18)
Illness, 25
Import-export, 11, 48, 74, 79, 84, (42)

Inbreeding, 17, 38–39

Liberty, keeping at, 51, 69, 91
Lonchura species, 89
Loriculus species, 77
Loss mutation, 41
Lutino varieties, 64

Masked lovebird, 18–37, (8, 11, 18–37)
Mauve varieties, 66–69

Nesting, 18–22, 27, 29–30, 52, 58, 70, 75–76, 78, 81, 88
Nestling, 23–24, 30, 58
Nyasa lovebird, 44–47, (11, 44–47)

Olive varieties, 66–69

Peat, 76, 81
Peach-faced lovebird, 54–69, (8, 10, 11, 12, 54–69)
Pets, lovebirds as, 21–23, 81, 91
Pied varieties, 38, 63, 65

Red-faced lovebird, 70–77, (10, 70–77)

Scaled varieties, 64
Sexing, 29, 54, 80

Temperature tolerance, 17, 22, 25, 31, 44, 48, 51, 60, 78, 90
Termitaria, 70

Voice, 22, 38, 47, 54, 74, 85

Water, 10, 27
White varieties, 34

Yellow varieties, 34, 38, 41, 63
Yellow-green varieties, 63

Two Nyasa lovebirds, Agapornis lilianae.

P9-EMG-386

Written by Megan Faulkner
Designed by Kat Peruyera
Cover and package designed by Bill Henderson

All rights reserved. No part of this publication may be reproduced,
or stored in a retrieval system, or transmitted in any form or by
any means, electronic, mechanical, photocopying, recording, or
otherwise, without written permission of Tangerine Press.

Copyright© 2015 Scholastic Inc.

an imprint of
SCHOLASTIC
www.scholastic.com

Scholastic and Tangerine Press and associated
logos are trademarks of Scholastic Inc.

Published by Tangerine Press, an imprint of Scholastic Inc.;
557 Broadway, New York, NY 10012

10 9 8 7 6 5 4 3 2 1
ISBN 978-0-545-85148-0

Printed and bound in Guangzhou, China

Photos ©: box paper scrap: t_kimura/iStockphoto; box water: ddbell/iStockphoto; box shark fins: SSSCCC/iStockphoto; box sharks: ap-images/iStockphoto; cover main: Mike Parry/Getty Images; back cover water: Maks Narodenko/Shutterstock, Inc.; 1 background: Andrey_Kuzmin/Shutterstock, Inc.; 2 main: Jim Abernethy/Getty Images; 3 top: www.Narchuk.com/Getty Images; 3 top paper: SCOTTCHAN/Shutterstock, Inc.; 3 center top: Creation/Shutterstock, Inc.; 3 center bottom: Jim Abernethy/Getty Images; 3 bottom: Chris Ross/Getty Images; 3 background: Jim Abernethy/Getty Images; 4 background: CoreyFord/iStockphoto; 4 bottom left: STILLFX/Shutterstock, Inc.; 4 bottom right: STILLFX/iStockphoto; 5 center: Catmando/Shutterstock, Inc.; 5 bottom teeth: Masterfile; 5 bottom left: donatas1205/Shutterstock, Inc.; 5 background: CoreyFord/iStockphoto; 6 background: Chris Ross/Getty Images; 6 bottom: moyogo/Wikimedia; 6 center left: Josh Humbert/Getty Images; 7 top: etraveler/iStockphoto; 7 bottom: bonishphotography/iStockphoto; 7 paper scrap: xpixel/Shutterstock, Inc.; 7 background: Chris Ross/Getty Images; 7 center: Hilton Mantooth; 8 main: Ruth Petzold/Getty Images; 9 top: David Jenkins/Robert Harding World Imagery/Corbis Images; 9 background: Ruth Petzold/Getty Images; 10 main: Education Images/UIG; 11 bottom right: STILLFX/Shutterstock, Inc.; 11 bottom left: NaluPhoto/iStockphoto; 11 background: Education Images/UIG; 12 main: Education Images/UIG/Getty Images; 13 center left: Greg Amptman/Shutterstock, Inc.; 13 center left photo frames: rangizzz/Shutterstock, Inc.; 13 center right: STILLFX/Shutterstock, Inc.; 13 bottom left: Matt9122/Shutterstock, Inc.; 13 bottom right: Devonyu/iStockphoto; 13 background: Education Images/UIG/Getty Images; 14 main: Karen Doody/Stocktrek Images/Getty Images; 15 center: MP cz/Shutterstock, Inc.; 15 bottom: ZWEID/iStockphoto; 15 main: Karen Doody/Stocktrek Images/Getty Images; 15 bottom photo frame: SCOTTCHAN/Shutterstock, Inc.; 16 main: stephaniki2/iStockphoto; 17 top: qldian/iStockphoto; 17 center: qldian/iStockphoto; 17 background: CAlleaume/iStockphoto; 17 background: stephaniki2/iStockphoto; 17 photo frames: SCOTTCHAN/Shutterstock, Inc.; 18 main: Matt9122/Shutterstock, Inc.; 19 center left: Shane Gross/Shutterstock, Inc.; 19 bottom left: ilbusca/iStockphoto; 19 bottom right: Matt9122/Shutterstock, Inc.; 19 background: Matt9122/Shutterstock, Inc.; 19 photo frame: SCOTTCHAN/Shutterstock, Inc.; 19 paper scrap: xpixel/Shutterstock, Inc.; 20 main: stephaniki2/iStockphoto; 21 top: UWphotographer/iStockphoto; 21 bottom right: JudiLen/iStockphoto; 21 bottom left: ShaneGross/iStockphoto; 21 background: stephaniki2/iStockphoto; 21 photo frames: SCOTTCHAN/Shutterstock, Inc.; 22 main: Alexander Sofonov/Barcroft Media/Getty Images; 23 center: Tui De Roy/Getty Images; 23 bottom: kamonchanok5211224102/iStockphoto; 23 background: Alexander Sofonov/Barcroft Media/Getty Images; 23 photo frame: SCOTTCHAN/Shutterstock, Inc.; 24 background: BryanToro/iStockphoto; 24 bottom: bonishphotography/iStockphoto; 24 photo frame: SCOTTCHAN/Shutterstock, Inc.; 25 center: Brian J. Skerry/Getty Images; 25 bottom: Mark Conlin/Getty Images; 25 background: BryanToro/iStockphoto; 25 photo frame: SCOTTCHAN/Shutterstock, Inc.; 26 main: Jim Abernethy/Getty Images; 27 bottom: NaluPhoto/iStockphoto; 27 background: Jim Abernethy/Getty Images; 27 photo frame: SCOTTCHAN/Shutterstock, Inc.; 28 background: dioch/Shutterstock, Inc.; 28 top: Entienou/iStockphoto; 28 center left: Stephen Frink/Getty Images; 28 center right: Steven Trainoff Ph.D./Getty Images; 29 top: atese/iStockphoto; 29 bottom: BlueRingMedia/Shutterstock, Inc.; 29 background: dioch/Shutterstock, Inc.; 30 background: Willyam Bradberry/Shutterstock, Inc.; 31 top: david olah/iStockphoto; 31 center top: bgton/iStockphoto; 31 center bottom: Fox Photos/Getty Images; 31 bottom left: Raphael Christinat/Shutterstock, Inc.; 31 bottom right: Anastasios71/Shutterstock, Inc.; 31 background: Willyam Bradberry/Shutterstock, Inc.; 31 photo frame: SCOTTCHAN/Shutterstock, Inc.; 32 background: Swimwitdafishes/iStockphoto; 32 paper scrap: xpixel/Shutterstock, Inc.

Attack and fatality statistics are from the International Shark Attack File (ISAF), Florida Museum
of Natural History, University of Florida. All statistics are for unprovoked attacks.

SHARK!

The word alone makes pulses race and eyes widen with fear. Images of massive mouths bearing down with razor-sharp, flesh-ripping teeth are imprinted on our minds. Though more humans are killed each year by vending machines—sharks, above any land predator—continue to be a source of terror and fascination.

Think You Know Sharks?

Though sharks have cruised the planet for 400 million years, we still have a lot to learn about these mysterious creatures. Sharks are challenging to study in the field because they are elusive, dangerous, and prone to migrating across enormous watery distances. Capturing specimens for observation isn't an option because most sharks die very quickly in captivity.

We still have so many unanswered questions about sharks! On the positive side, scientists are sharing fascinating new discoveries about sharks every day. Our journey toward understanding these amazing beasts is just beginning!

MEGAL

Although a face-to-face encounter with a hungry great white is most people's worst nightmare, modern apex predators are mere whispers of their forefish.

During the 14th to 17th century, gigantic triangular fossils as large as a man's hand were found embedded in rock. Believed to be the petrified tongues of dragons and snakes, these "tongue stones" were thought to be an antidote for poisons and toxins. Noblemen and royalty wore them as pendants or kept them in their pockets as good-luck charms. These were not dragon teeth. They were shark teeth belonging to Megalodon—perhaps the most fearsome predator to ever exist on Earth.

In its day, Megalodon cruised the oceans eating giant sea turtles like potato chips and attacking whales as if they were chew toys.

Rumors persist that Megalodon isn't extinct but is secretly trolling the depths of our oceans. Although it's thrilling to imagine such a beast is still out there, scientific facts prove otherwise. When the water temperature changed and their food sources died out, so too did Megalodon.

ODON (Carcharodon megalodon)

Lived:
15.9 million–2.6 million years ago during the Cenozoic Era (middle Miocene to end of Pliocene)

Claim to Fame:
Largest marine predator EVER

Size:
Length: Estimates range from 52–80 ft (16–24 m)
Weight: Estimates range from 53–114 tons (48–103 metric tons)

Distinguishing Characteristics:
A huge, stocky body with a giant mouth full of enormous teeth. Picture a mouth with fins.

Habitat:
Megalodon is believed to have hunted all the oceans in a wide range of marine environments–no region was spared its voracious appetite!

Diet:
Whales, dolphins, sea turtles, land creatures taking a dip

Hunting Style:
1. Open mouth
2. Swallow prey

Natural Predators:
NONE

A shark loses and replaces around 35,000 teeth over its lifespan.

Without a skeleton, scientists can only make educated guesses about Megalodon's size based on the similarity of the fossilized teeth to those of today's great white. Reaching lengths more than 7 in (17.78 cm), Megalodon teeth are the same shape and have the same serrated edges as the great white. Scientists have differing theories about Megalodon's size. At this point, we just don't know which one is correct.

Because shark skeletons are made of cartilage (the flexible connective tissue that makes your ears bendy), and cartilage breaks down over time, all that remains of prehistoric sharks are their teeth.

THE DANGER ZONE

Most unprovoked shark attacks happen off the Atlantic coast of Florida in the United States. Australia has the second highest number of attacks, followed by South Africa. These rankings are not concrete, however, because attacks in South Africa are not documented as they are elsewhere. Despite having the highest number of recorded attacks, only about 16 attacks occur per year in the United States, and one fatality every two years.

Map of World's Unprovoked Shark Attacks 1580–2014:

- 500 or more
- 200-499
- 40-199
- 1-39

Last updated Feb 20, 2014, International Shark Attack File, Florida Museum of Natural History, University of Florida

Though movies such as *Jaws* and shows from *Shark Week* make it look like sharks are hungry for human blood, the truth is we don't have the fat-to-bone ratio that a shark looks for in a tasty snack. Most shark attacks on humans are a case of mistaken identity. Unfortunately, such powerful jaws and sharp teeth mean a tiny taste test can result in fatal or disfiguring bites to a human body.

CAUTION!

SHARKS!

Human-Shark encounters usually fall into one of three categories:

The "Hit and Run" Attack: The most common type of encounter; the shark mistakes a human for prey and takes a bite, realizes its mistake, then releases and retreats. Often the victim does not even see the shark.

The "Bump and Bite" Attack: The shark circles the victim and gives it an exploratory bump, then moves in for multiple strikes. These are often severe wounds resulting in death. The motive is likely feeding or antagonistic behavior rather than mistaken identity.

The "Sneak" Attack: A series of vicious strikes with no warning bump.

Profile of the average shark victim

The longer you spend in shark-infested waters, the higher your chance of being attacked. For this reason, males between the ages of 18 and 35 who spend a lot of time surfing and swimming along the coast of Florida are the most likely to have an encounter with a shark.

A Shark Attack Story

Hilton Mantooth, a 16-year-old surfer, was never really concerned about being bitten by a shark, even though he was swimming in shark-infested waters. "Sure. I've seen them out there. I've even been chased, but my friends and I didn't really think about it," he said. On one fateful day, Hilton and his friends were surfing the inlet at New Smyrna Beach, Fla. He was sitting on his board with his feet dangling in the water when what he thinks was a blacktip shark attacked him from underneath. The shark bit his foot twice before deciding that he wasn't a meal. Hilton says, "I'll definitely get back in the water as soon as I can. The shark was just doing what animals do— feeding. They need to be respected. After all, I was in their home."

GREAT WHITE SHARK

(Carcharodon carcharias)

As the most famous, most feared, and most awe-inspiring of the shark family, the great white needs little introduction. To say it is top of the food chain is an understatement. The largest predatory fish on the planet is a lean, mean killing machine. Averaging 15 ft (5 m) in length and reaching speeds up to 35 mph (50 kmh), the great white's equally impressive brain coordinates brute force with sensory information to take down its prey of choice. New research shows the great white is more social than was believed. Complex relationships exist between sharks that

Great whites may be the most frightening shark, but they are not the largest. That honor goes to the whale shark (*Rhincodon typus*), which averages 45 ft (14 m) in length and weighs around 47,000 lbs (21.5 mt). That's one BIG fish!

With a single bite, a great white can take in up to 31 lbs. (14 kg) of flesh!

Claim to Fame:
Biggest threat to humans

Size:
Average length: 13-17 ft (4-5 m)
Average weight: 4,000-7,000 lbs (680-1,100 kg)

Body Count:
Total attacks: 279
Fatal attacks: 78

Distinguishing Characteristics:
Great whites have a gray to gray-brown upper body and white belly. They have large, serrated, triangular teeth.

Habitat:
Worldwide in temperate and subtropical oceans, with a preference for cooler waters. Inshore waters around rocky reefs and islands, and often near seal colonies.

Diet:
Marine mammals, fish, sea birds

Hunting Style:
The "spy-hopping" technique involves lifting its head above the water to look for prey. Approaching its prey from below at speeds up to 35 mph (50 km) per hour, the great white partially or completely clears the water, a behavior known as breaching. Disabling its prey with the first powerful bite, the great white retreats until the victim is weakened from blood loss, then returns to devour the remains.

Natural Predators:
Orca

Lifespan:
70+ years

BULL SHARK

(Carcharhinus leucas)

hough great whites are #1 in terms of human attacks, the bull shark is at least as much of a threat to humans. Aside from their brute strength and awesome bite power, bulls can cross from saltwater to freshwater with ease. This sneaky ability gives them access to freshwater rivers and estuaries where humans aren't expecting them, contributing to a high number of unprovoked attacks.

Bite marks from bull sharks have been found on hippopotamuses in Africa's Zambezi River. They are fearless!

Claim to Fame:
Freshwater/saltwater switch hitter

Size:
Average length:
7.5 ft (2.2 m)
Average weight:
209–290 lbs (95–130 kg)

Body Count
Total attacks: 93
Fatal attacks: 67

Distinguishing Characteristics:
"Bull" comes from their stocky shape, blunt snout, small eyes, and aggressive, unpredictable behavior.

Habitat:
Worldwide in the warm shallow waters around coasts and rivers, freshwater estuaries and rivers, and brackish shallows.

Diet:
Bony fish and other sharks (including other bull sharks), turtles, birds, dolphins, terrestrial mammals, crustaceans, and stingrays

Hunting Style:
Bulls are primarily solo hunters. They prefer to attack in murky water so their prey cannot see them coming. The "bump-and-bite" method is often used.

Natural Predators:
Tiger sharks, great whites, larger bull sharks, saltwater crocodiles

Lifespan:
12–16 years

the 2 ...2 ...son.

Bull sharks will throw up their stomach contents to distract predators. As the predator moves in to eat the regurgitated food, the bull shark has an opportunity to escape.

ed
are
't
eir

she

that

cord breaking teen

TIGER SHARK

(Galeocerdo cuvier)

The tiger shark is known for the variety of its diet. Some sharks are picky eaters, focusing their efforts on seals and other favorites, but not the tiger shark. Plump sea bird or tin can, juicy squid or suit of armor—it's all in a day's lunch for a tiger shark! In addition to being a voracious eater, the tiger shark prowls a broad range of habitats—shallow reefs, harbors, and canals—increasing the potential for human encounters.

Claim to Fame:
Garbage can of the sea

Size:
Average length: 12 ft (4 m)
Average weight: 849–1,400 lbs (385–635 kg)

Body Count:
Total attacks: 101
Fatal attacks: 28

Distinguishing Characteristics:
Dark black spots and vertical stripes down the body.

Habitat:
Worldwide in temperate and tropical waters, with the exception of the Mediterranean Sea. Murky waters in coastal areas and open oceans.

Diet:
Crustaceans, marine mammals, fish, jellyfish, squid, turtles, sea snakes, smaller sharks, various inedible man-made items

Hunting Style:
The tiger shark circles its prey and investigates by prodding it with its snout. When attacking, the shark often eats its prey whole, although larger prey is eaten in large bites and finished over time.

Natural Predators:
Larger tiger sharks

Lifespan:
12+ years

Weird Diet

The following items have been found inside the stomachs of tiger sharks:
A polar bear, reindeer, musical instruments, license plates, tires, a chicken coop with chickens, suit of armor, fur coat, barrel of nails, driver's license, porcupine, dogs (some wearing collars), video camera, horse head, bag of money, pigs, sheep, Barbie doll, tools, bottles of wine, 16th-century medallion, cannonball and other live munitions, bag of potatoes, jewelry, pair of pants, empty wallet, hyenas, monkeys, boat cushions, unopened can of salmon, cats, can of peas, human parts.

SAND TIGER SHARK

(Carcharias Taurus)

With its wide mouth and haphazard teeth, the sand tiger is known for its deceptively fearsome looks and docile personality. Reluctant to engage with humans unless provoked, the sand tiger is one of the few species of shark able to survive in captivity. Its laid-back personality, menacing appearance, and ability to thrive in captivity makes it the most likely species to be seen in an aquarium.

Claim to Fame:
Shark most in need of orthodontics

Size:
Average length:
6.5–10 ft (2–3 m)
Average weight:
200–350 lbs (90–160 kg)

Body Count:
Total attacks: 29
Fatal attacks: 2

Distinguishing Characteristics:
The sand tiger has a gray-brown back and pale underside. Adults have reddish-brown spots. Long, narrow, sharp teeth impale fish.

Habitat:
Sandy coastal waters, estuaries, shallow bays, and rocky or tropical reefs

Diet:
Small bony fish, rays, skates, squid, crustaceans, smaller sharks

Hunting Style:
Taking a gulp of air at the surface and holding it in its stomach to stay buoyant, the virtually motionless sand tiger silently glides up beside its prey, then attacks with a quick sideways snap. Yikes!

Natural Predators:
Larger sand tiger sharks

Lifespan:
15+ years

A sand tiger shark in captivity

BLACKTIP
SHARK

(Carcharhinus limbatus)

ast and energetic, the nimble blacktip is known for leaping above the water and performing multiple spins in the air in pursuit of prey. These spins are the spectacular finale of a feeding run. The shark corkscrews through a school of fish grabbing as many fish as it can at a very high speed. The momentum created propels the shark completely

Claim to Fame:
Most acrobatic

Size:
Average length:
5–9 ft (1.5–2.7 m)
Average weight:
66–220 lbs (30–100 kg)

Body Count:
Total attacks: 28
Fatal attacks: 1

Distinguishing Characteristics:
Named for its black-trimmed fins, the blacktip has a long, pointy snout and distinct white band along its flank.

Habitat:
Coastal and subtropical waters around the world including brackish waters. Waters less than 100 ft deep (30 m), muddy bays, island lagoons, and drop-offs near coral reefs, mangrove swamps

Diet:
Small schooling fish, boney fish, rays and skates, smaller sharks, crustaceans, and the odd cephalopod

Hunting Style:
Blacktips are social and live and hunt in groups. Timid by nature, they become aggressive and competitive around prey resulting in a feeding frenzy.

Natural Predators:
Larger sharks

Lifespan:
12+ years

The blacktip performs a weird dance when threatened. It swims toward the threat then turns away, all the while rolling from side to side, lowering its pectoral fins, tilting its head and tail upward, and making sideways biting motions. (Try this next time you go swimming.)

GREAT HAMMER-HEAD

(Sphyrna mokarran)

Of the nine species of hammerhead sharks, the great hammerhead is the largest. Its unique hammer-shaped head (called a *cephalofoil*) makes it the easiest shark to identify. A solo hunter by night, by day the hammerhead gathers in schools 100-strong.

Claim To Fame:
Weirdest-looking head

Size:
Average length:
13–20 ft (4–6 m)
Average weight:
500–1,000 lbs
(230–450 kg)

Body Count:
Total attacks: 21
Fatal attacks: 2

Distinguishing Characteristics:
Large size, flat rectangular head, prominent dorsal fin.

Habitat:
Continental shelves and lagoons in coastal, warm, temperate, and tropical waters

Diet:
Stingrays, fish, squid, octopus, crustaceans, other sharks and even their own young

Hunting Style:
The hammerhead swims directly above the ocean floor, swaying its flattened head from side to side in a sweeping motion to detect the electric signature of stingrays hiding beneath the sand. When a ray is located, the hammerhead delivers a hard blow from above, then pins it to the seafloor and chomps off each wing so it can't escape.

Natural Predators:
Larger hammerheads, bull sharks

Lifespan:
20–30 years

The uniquely shaped head is specially adapted to hunt the hammerhead's favorite meal: stingrays. The broad, flat area is densely packed with ampullae of Lorenzini—the sensory receptors all sharks use to detect the electromagnetic impulses of prey. The wide-set eye placement gives the hammerhead a greater range of vision to better scan the ocean floor for stingrays hiding in the sand.

BLUE SHARK

(Prionace glauca)

With its indigo-colored back, vibrant blue sides, and white underbelly, the blue shark is one of the easiest sharks to identify. These sleek, fast, deep-water dwellers are likely responsible for the deaths of shipwreck and air crash victims. Naturally curious, they are known to circle swimmers or divers for

Claim To Fame:
Best-looking shark

Size:
Average length:
6-10 ft (1.8-3 m)
Average weight:
60-120 lbs (27-54 kg)

Body Count:
Total attacks: 13*
Fatal attacks: 4
*Due to its deep, open-water habitat, blue sharks are likely responsible for the consumption of shipwrecked and downed-aircraft survivors. These multiple-casualty incidents are not included in global shark attack logs, so no one knows the actual human body count for the blue shark.

Distinguishing Characteristics:
Bright blue upper body; large eyes; long conical snout; very long, pointed pectoral fins

Habitat:
Deep waters of the world's temperate and tropical oceans

Diet:
Blue sharks prefer squid but will settle for fish, smaller sharks, and seabirds.

Hunting Style:
Like wolves, blue sharks are known to hunt in a cooperative pack. They work together to herd schools of fish into the shallows for easier feeding.

Natural Predators:
California sea lions, great whites, tiger shark, shortfin makos

Lifespan:
20+ years

BRONZE WHALER

(Carcharhinus brachyurus)

The name "whaler" dates back to the 19th century when these sharks would gather around the carcasses of harpooned whales hanging alongside

Claim to Fame:
The summer swimmer

Size:
Average length:
11 ft. (3.3 m)
Average weight:
672 lbs (305 kg)

Body Count:
Total attacks: 30
Fatal attacks: 1

Distinguishing Characteristics:
The bronze whaler's slim, streamlined body is a metallic olive-gray color with a pink tinge on the top and white on the bottom. The color darkens slightly toward the fin tips. It has a long, pointed snout and narrow, hook-shaped upper teeth.

Habitat:
Worldwide in warm, temperate, and subtropical waters and shallow coastline regions, freshwater and brackish areas of large rivers to shallow bays and estuaries

Diet:
Cephalopods, bony fish, cartilaginous fish

Hunting Style:
Bronze whalers hunt in groups up to 100.

Natural Predators:
Larger sharks

Lifespan:
25–30 years

SHORTFIN MAKO

(Isurus oxyrinchus)

With its dizzying speed, superb jumping abilities, and high intelligence, the mako is a fearsome predator. Reaching cruising speeds of 25 mph (40km) punctuated with bursts up to 46 mph (74 km), the mako can breach the water at heights of 30 ft (9 m) or higher! Angry makos have been known to attack and leap right into boats.

Claim to Fame:
Highest jumper

Size:
Average length:
10-12.5 ft (3-4 m)
Average weight:
672 lbs (305 kg)

Body Count:
Total attacks: 10
Fatal attacks: 1

Distinguishing Characteristics:
Makos have a brilliant, metallic-blue upper body. The shortfin mako can be identified by its white chin and snout. (Longfin makos have a blue chin and snout.)

Habitat:
Open water in temperate and tropical seas worldwide.

Diet:
Cephalopods, bony fish, other sharks, dolphins, seabirds

Hunting Style:
The mako swims below its prey, hovering in its blind spot, then suddenly lunges upward to capitalize on the element of surprise, often breaching the water.

Natural Predators:
Larger makos

Lifespan:
30 years

"Mako" is the Maori word for *shark*.

WHITETIP

(Carcharhinus longimanus)

an you imagine surviving a shipwreck or plane crash into the ocean, only to be eaten by a shark? Thanks to the whitetip, many such "survivors" quickly become dinner. Like the blue shark, the whitetip lives in open water and is quick to arrive on the scene of a possible meal. Stubborn in their pursuit of prey, whitetips work themselves into a feeding frenzy as they compete for food.

Claim to Fame:
Frenzied feeder

Size:
Average length:
6–10 ft (2–3 m)
Average weight:
370 lbs (168 kg)

Body Count:
Total attacks: 10*
Fatal attacks: 3
*Due to its habit of eating sailors and others lost at sea, there is no accurate body count for the white tip because multiple-casualty incidents are not included in global shark attack logs.

Distinguishing Characteristics:
The whitetip's rounded fins and long, winglike pectoral and dorsal fins are easily identifiable. The fins have white tips that may be mottled.

Habitat:
Open water in temperate and tropical seas worldwide.

Diet:
Cephalopods, bony fish, other sharks, dolphins, seabirds

Hunting Style:
Whitetip feeding methods include biting into groups of fish and swimming through schools of tuna with an open mouth.

Though generally slow-moving, the whitetip will become aggressive in pursuit of prey. With the arrival of more whitetips at the scene, the competitors quickly work themselves into a vicious feeding frenzy.

Natural Predators:
Larger sharks

Lifespan:
Up to 22 years

During World War II, the *Nova Scotia*—a steamship carrying about 1,000 passengers—was sunk by a German submarine near South Africa. With only 192 survivors, many deaths were attributed to the whitetip.

ANATOMY OF A SHARK

Teeth

Shark teeth are attached to the gums rather than the jaw. Several backup rows exist so when a tooth is lost, another moves forward immediately to take its place. Shape depends on the shark's diet. Mollusk- and crustacean-eaters have blunt teeth for crushing; fish-eaters have thin, needlelike teeth to spear and grip; and meat-eaters have pointed, triangular-shaped teeth with tiny serrations for ripping through flesh.

Shape

Most shark bodies are rounded in the center and taper at each end like a bullet or torpedo, a hydrodynamic shape that increases speed.

Dermal Denticles

A shark's skin is made up of dermal denticles. These are tiny scales similar to teeth. Like teeth, each denticle has a layer of enamel and includes dentine and a pulp cavity. Denticles completely cover the shark's body and act as an external skeleton. Muscles are attached directly to the denticles, which makes them more efficient and saves energy. Denticles streamline the body to improve speed and provide protection from predators.

Fins

Most sharks have four to five fins:

Pectoral: Located near the head, the pectoral fins are used to lift and steer while swimming.

Pelvic: The pelvic fin sits behind the pectoral fin(s) and aids in stabilization.

Dorsal Fin: This is the fin that sticks out of the water when a shark swims close to the surface. It is also used for stabilization.

Anal Fin: Situated on the rear underside of the shark, these fins provide further stabilization.

Caudal Fin: Also called the tail fin, it provides the most thrust to propel the shark through the water. It has upper and lower lobes that vary in shape and size between types of shark. Most of the thrust comes from the top lobe.

Smell is the most important of a shark's senses. Sharks inhale water through their noistrils and filter it through the olfactory sacs. Signals sent to the brain allow the shark to determine the presence of prey. It is said the great white can smell one drop of blood in 10 billion drops of water from more than 300 feet (91 m) away.

Gills

Like other fish, sharks breathe with gills instead of lungs. Water enters the shark's mouth and flows over the gills, where oxygen is absorbed into the bloodstream to be pumped throughout the body. The water then exits through five to seven gill slits on each side of the head.

Spiracles

Some sharks have openings above their eyes that draw oxygenated water into their gills. This means the shark can breathe while lying motionless on the sea floor. To keep water flowing over their gills, sharks without spiracles must move continuously.

Ampullae of Lorenzini

Small groups of sensitive cells under the skin in the shark's head detect the vibrations and electrical fields of fish and other prey.

Countershading

The upper half of the shark is dark to blend with the deeper water beneath when viewed from above. The lower half is white so it blends with the lighter water near the surface when viewed from below. This helps disguise the shark from predators and prey.

Nictitating Membrane

This translucent, tough membrane is a third eyelid that covers and protects the eye from damage during attacks. Not all sharks have them. The great white, for instance, must roll its eyes backward in their sockets for protection just before striking.

Lateral Line

This line of sensory cells along the shark's body detects changes in the movement of surrounding water. Erratic water movements indicate the presence of prey.

WHAT'S INSIDE

Skeleton

The skeleton of a shark is made of cartilage. This flexible connective tissue allows the shark to bend and twist easily. It is half the weight of bone, which lowers the shark's body mass, meaning less energy is used to propel it through the water.

Liver

A shark's liver is its largest internal organ. The liver stores a lot of oil, which provides an energy reserve between meals. Sharks have been known to survive on their internal oil as long as a year!

Digestion

Food moves from the mouth to the J-shaped stomach, where it can sit for long periods without being digested. Sharks will barf out undigestible items, but some species can completely turn the stomach inside out through their mouth, rinse it with seawater, and return it to its normal inside place.

A WORLD WITHOUT SHARKS

Despite a reputation as bloodthirsty man-eaters, sharks on average kill only three or four humans a year. Meanwhile, humans kill an estimated 100 million sharks each year—or 12,000 sharks per hour. Six thousand sharks were killed while you read this book.

Here are some of the reasons:

Overfishing:
Commercial fisheries harvest sharks for their meat and fins.

Sharkfin Soup:
An estimated 75 percent of sharks are killed each year for their fins alone. A symbol of wealth and prosperity, this traditional Chinese soup is served at weddings and special occasions. Because only the fin is valuable to hunters, it is sliced off, and the shark is thrown back into the ocean to die slowly from suffocation or a predatory attack. This horrific method is called *finning*.

Habitat Destruction:
Development and pollution push shark populations out of areas long used for feeding and nurseries.

Skin:
Shark leather is used for purses, bags, shoes, boots, coats, belts, wallets, car interiors, watch straps, gloves, gun holsters, and phone cases.

Bycatch:
Sharks become tangled in the nets, lines, trawls, and fish traps of commercial fisheries.

Sport Fishing and Trophy Hunting:
Due to their size, rarity, and fearsome reputation, sharks are greatly prized by trophy hunters.

Public Aquariums:
A live shark on display makes a lot of money for zoos and aquariums. Sadly, most captive sharks die within a year, even in the most state-of-the-art aquariums.

Public Fear:
Due to media exaggeration of sharks' threat to humans, the fear of sharks among the general population is so great, the mere sighting of a single shark can trigger an extensive cull (hunt) of the local shark population. Sharks also die from getting tangled in the shark barrier nets installed around swimming areas.

GLOSSARY

Apex predator—Predators with no natural predators of their own. They reside at the top of the food chain and have a crucial role in maintaining the health of their ecosystems.

Cartilaginous fish—Fish with a flexible skeleton made of cartilage instead of bone.

ISAF—International Shark Attack File

Serration —Jagged edges on a tooth that improve the ability to slice through meat